1

Running with the Horses
a memoir of travel, racetracks, & foods

Arlene S. Bice

Running with the Horses, a memoir of *travel, racetracks, & foods*
Copyright ©2022 Arlene S. Bice

ISBN: 9798420311325

In Memory of Angelo Falvo

PurpleStone Press

Introduction

I didn't match Angelo's passion for horses but was a keen observer of the horses, people, places, and everything around the horses. He loved going to the track. He said the races relaxed him and let him forget the troubles he carried. That alone amazed me. Relax? At the track? When horses are thundering down to the finish line? And you have a bet on one of them? Wow. What a guy!

My path to the racetrack crossed many other paths over the 15 years that I accompanied Angelo to horse racing tracks. Some were places long familiar to him. Being a barber by trade with nothing else to do that interested him on a Monday when his shop was closed, he went to the races. Yet he only went to nearby tracks (within 30 miles) even though he heard his customers (all men) talk about the faraway tracks. That changed after we met. He found a traveler in me to match his own.

I never saw him bet more than he had set aside in one pocket. He rarely went home with that pocket empty. I never asked if he won or lost and he never told. I went because it was important to him for me to be there. He liked having me by his side.

I was a novice at the beginning of the racing journey and not greatly knowledgeable when it ended. Yet I did absorb bits and pieces by observing and listening whenever I heard the word *horse* mentioned. I picked a few winners too, mostly by devotion to the feminine entering as jockeys, an uncommon situation at that time. I also followed my instinct for the long shots and the racing form for the favorites. These were pre-internet years when information was not readily available at my fingertips.

All the back history of these tracks was not known to me at the time. Much came later. I didn't know anything about the sport at all. As a teenager, the horse was a beautiful, gallant figure that intrigued me. I spent earned babysitting money to build an extensive and costly collection of ceramic, porcelain, and even metal horses. All were destroyed by a flood in our basement in my early years of marriage.

Jewelry with horses or horseshoes depicted were given to me as gifts. I still have all of those. In high school art class I poured a mold, baked, and painted a beautiful black horse head. It showed the elegance and pride of the equine. As an adult it was a joy to watch their performance at the track as well as the jockeys.

Travel, history, and foods were important to me which made Angelo the perfect travel mate even when racetrack attendance was not planned. He never discouraged me from exploring a place even when he had no interest. He sat in the car with a glass of wine and read the newspaper. No rush. No fuss.

We were also both food aficionados. We enjoyed making wine, cooking, canning tomatoes, preserving peppers, and eggplant together. His palate was just as curious as mine when it came to tasting foods of other cultures. We both delighted in dining out or inviting friends in. We shared a curious mind, a thirst for faraway places with strange sounding names and foods prepared in an unfamiliar manner and served in pleasant surroundings.

For a brief moment Angelo and I considered buying a percentage of a racehorse. Enthusiasts can purchase shares in a horse of 1% up to 20%. If a horse is bought for $40,000 a 2.5% share would cost $1,000. Each share is responsible for 2.5% of the stall rental, vet bills, training bills, etc. If our horse won a race, we would receive 2.5% earnings of the purse. (This information came from the internet.) There are some good websites that give accurate advice and information on buying shares in a racehorse.

Angelo was knowledgeable about the performance of racehorses and some of the men who owned and trained them. Several were faithful customers. In those days women didn't go to his barber shop for haircuts (He did cut mine. He was good.) so he had no inside track (forgive the pun) about female jockeys.

We decided not to buy into any horse, but to just enjoy the races as we enjoyed everything else we did together.

Enjoy,
Arlene S. Bice

"The profession of book writing makes horse racing seem like a solid, stable business."

John Steinbeck

"A horse doesn't know whether the rider on his back wears a dress or pants away from the track."

Diane Crump

"Books on horse racing subjects have never done well, and I am told that publishers had come to think of them as the literary version of box office poison."

Laura Hillenbrand

Contents

A Few Definitions

ACROSS THE BOARD: A bet on a horse to win, place, and show. If the horse wins, the player collects three ways; if second, two ways, and if third, one way, losing the win and place bets.

ALSO-RAN: A horse who finishes out of the money.

BOARD: Totalisator board on which odds, betting pools and other information is displayed.

CLOSER: A horse who runs best in the latter part of the race.

COLORS: Racing jacket and cap worn by riders to denote the owner(s) of a horse, also called silks.

DAILY DOUBLE: Type of wager calling for the selection of winners of two consecutive races, usually the first and second.

ITB: Inter Track Betting: Wagering on a simulcast of a race from another track within the state.

PARIMUTUEL: A form of wagering that originated in France in which all money bet is divided up among those who have winning tickets, after taxes, takeout and other deductions are made.

PICK SIX: A type of wager in which the winners of all the included races must be selected.

QUINELLA: Wager in which first two finishers must be picked, but payoff is made no matter which of the two wins and which runs second.

STAKES RACE: At least part of the prize money is put up by horse owners such as entry fees.

Chapter 1
Yonkers Harness Raceway
Yonkers, New York

On this night in 1982 I had no clue where we were or where the race track was located. I noticed the traffic pattern was far different from my neighborhood. I lived and worked in rural New Egypt, central New Jersey surrounded by race horse farms, as in raising and training. It was said that New Jersey had more horses than Texas.

On this night Angelo was driving to Yonkers Raceway. Our first sojourn into the horse racing world together. He drove, I looked out the window at cars zooming by and cutting in front of us. *Crazy New York drivers* I thought as we moved along in this nighttime excursion. It took us nearly two hours to get there and the same time to get home. Nutsy.

We were both in our 40s and dating for a month or so. My children were grown. I really didn't know anything about his life except electricity zapped between us on the first day we met and continued each time I saw him. I knew he felt the same sparking connection.

Angelo was a barber whose shop was a block from where I worked part-time tending bar to help my friend Herman who was recuperating from a stroke. I was there during his busiest hours after leaving my real estate office at 2:00 p.m. Each day the same people, more or less, came in like they were stepping into their dad's house to see their gathered friends. It felt like hosting a cocktail party, only I went off duty after four hours with my pockets overflowing with dollar bills. Five days a week. It was a boon to my budget like attending my own sweet sixteen birthday party where all my relatives gave me money gifts instead of sweaters.

As bartenders did, I noticed Angelo was well liked and respected by Herman and everyone else in the daily group. The men came from various backgrounds and jobs. There were iron workers, detectives, a newspaperman, accountants, and even a police captain among them. Their response to Angelo went a long way in my judging his character.

Every time he came in, he did a hale and hearty "Hi peoples!" It was always a few minutes after 5 p.m. He carried a head full of gleaming silver hair, sun tanned skin and a smile that lit up the entire room. He never stayed more than a half hour. The other patrons looked forward to seeing him enter, even the ones who had difficulty cutting through his heavy Italian accent. Cheerfulness swept in the door with him. Four months later he invited me to dinner. We were practically inseparable after that date.

Angelo gave me no hints about horse racing. I knew nothing about racetracks, but on this first night at the track, I was trying to impress him by dressing up and foolish enough to wear high heels. Duh.

We arrived at Yonkers and saw masses of people charging into the grandstand like someone was giving away hundred dollar bills, completely unaware of anyone around them. They focused on getting to where they wanted to be, looking for the action. I walked a step behind Angelo, following wherever he led me. I was horrified that I might lose him and be stranded in this place, alone and unable to find my way home. It didn't take long to realize my high heels were not the best shoes to wear. It was a lesson learned but I suffered the whole night first. I'm sure I walked several miles before the night was over! The horses had it far better and more comfortable with their metal horse shoes than I did.

When we found seats in the grandstand Angelo leaped up and headed for the betting windows. He never said, "I'll be right back" or "wait here while I place a bet" or anything else. He was so engrossed in reading the horse stats that he never explained a thing to me, just handed me a racing program.

I waited and glanced at the program, properly called the Daily Racing Form. There were a lot of numbers and fine print and other print that could have been hieroglyphics for all I could tell.

After resting my feet on the seat back in front of me for an hour and listening to my stomach grumble, I announced, "I'm going to wander around." I *think* I heard an *okay* in response.

I found the concession stand and tried to read the offerings on the board. It was crowded and these New Yorkers knew what they wanted and they wanted me out of the way so they could reach the food counter and get it.

Whew! I happily settled on a knish. I had not eaten a knish in years so I enjoyed every bite. I doubted anyone in Plumsted Township knew about the savory Jewish hand-held pie filled with mashed potatoes, onions, and who knew what else. The flaky crust was made with cream cheese and butter. This delicious baked goodie just improved coming to the racetrack by 100% in my eyes.

After savoring each crumb, I kicked through a multitude of losing tickets covering the floor like piles of dried leaves on a late October walk in Princeton. I was horrified! It was littering that could be easily avoided by using the many huge trash cans placed everywhere! My mind couldn't wrap around the carelessness of these people! There were 30,000 people with many losing tickets each! Everyone just dropped their tickets to the floor!

While I was despairing of the poor manners at the track, the lights blinked and blinked some more. The tote board lit up in bright lights as the announcer said loud and clear, "Hold onto your tickets, folks. The judges are calling for an inquiry."

Many folks who thought they lost the race threw their tickets down into the mess on the floor. Some had torn theirs in half before tossing them away! Guys scrambled the piles looking for their tickets! It was like looking for a particular red leaf on the sidewalk where the streets were lined with maple and oak trees.

Everyone seemed to stop breathing and stared at the tote board. What a mess! It must have lasted a few minutes but seemed like an hour! I watched their facial expressions. The original win locked in and the winning payoffs were up. The tickets found were again tossed away in disgust! It was interesting to watch those expressions. I closed my ears to their mutters. They weren't nice.

With all the theatrics going on around me, I finally stepped into line after watching and listening to how others placed their bets. I stuttered a bit as I put my $2 into the little opening under the bars on the window. I wanted to chat a bit with the clerk, maybe ask a question.

But I waited too long to get in line. The bettors behind me were edgy and nervous about making the window on time before it closed and they got shut out. Everyone waited until the last minute because the odds kept changing. I could hear and feel their moving weight from one foot to the other. They were silently telling me to hurry up! The racing forms rattled and the gamblers began to breathe heavily. They had a winning bet to place! Pressure. Geez.

Why don't they get in line earlier? Guess it was time for me to get into mode and become one with the crowd.

At least I recognized one name in the racing form, Stanley Dancer. I learned later that he was a popular, winning harness racing driver at Yonkers. It was cool, thinking of the photos of his winning horses, names and winning records decorating the walls of the American House Tavern and restaurant where I worked a few years ago. He was well-liked and respected in his home town. I never saw him there because I worked days and he came in on occasion for dinner at night. He was a living legend.

Finally it was time to leave. It seemed like we had walked a mile from the car to the building. Inside we walked up and down the bleachers in the grandstand, walked down to the trackside rail, back up to place bets, down the steps to get back to our seats, and eventually return to the parking lot that looked like a wholesale internation-al car dealership! There was a huge sea of cars and our car was some-where in the middle. I was happy when we found it. I kept picturing 30,000 cars trying to leave at the same time. So I was glad we didn't stay until the end.

The famous Seabiscuit won the Scarsdale Handicap here in 1936, giving hope, as he did, to many Americans suffering during these depression years. The country watched this unknown horse become an unexpected champion and they related to him. He became a National symbol that the country's down-and-out-people would follow hoping they could also survive and become successful.

Chapter 2
Philadelphia Park
Bensalem, Pennsylvania

"I'm a barber. I'm closed on Mondays and what else is there to do on a Monday?"

That was the answer I got when I asked Angelo, shortly after we met and began dating, *why horse racing*?

Philadelphia Park was across the Delaware River from his Bordentown (NJ) shop and northeast of Philly so it became his place to go on Monday afternoons when the racing calendar was open. He'd been going for many years before we met.

Philadelphia Park began as Keystone Racetrack. It opened in November '74 relieving Liberty Bell Park of its thorough-bred racing so they could return to their original program of harness racing. When Keystone was purchased in 1984 by ITB, it renamed the track Philadelphia Park and sported a desirable turf course.

They installed a new way to please the trackmen that couldn't get there, called Phonebet. Fans could set up an account and place bets by telephone. It was so successful that New Jersey Racing Commission eventually stepped in and stopped New Jersey residents from utilizing this feature. Ah, jealousy, politics, money, and tying up the little guy.

My next excursion to the racing circle was on a Monday afternoon (I wangled Mondays off by finding a part time bartender fo fill in for me at Herman's.) shortly after the Yonkers trip. I was still wide-eyed and eager to learn about this sport that intertwined Angelo's life.

This time when I charged through the gate, I wore sensible shoes, still following Angelo. His attention was already on the horses. He handed me the program for the day and drifted off. Again, he wasn't about to take time to explain anything to me, so I did what I always did, I read.

The Daily Racing Form was a slender booklet full of information about what type of race, what jockeys were riding, some stats about the horse and some info on the jockeys. I watched everyone else lined up at the window to place a bet, I eavesdropped and copied the way it was said and nervously handed over my $2 bet to win.

Before the end of the afternoon, you'd think I was an old pro. I spent $10 and came home with $10 less than I started with. Zero gain. You'd think that losing money would deter me, but I liked new experiences.

Years ago someone told me, as I tended bar in New Egypt, which was surrounded by race horse stables, that it was best to lose the first time a newbie goes to the track. They have less chance of getting hooked. I had no fear of that happening. I worked too hard for my money and there wasn't a lot of it to spread around. I wasn't hooked on the horses but I *was* hooked on Angelo. So horse racing became part of my life.

Philadelphia Park was the thoroughbred track we went to more often than any other when the horses were running there. The Park closed down for certain months of the calendar year. Angelo said, "I like being here on Mondays because everyone else is working while I watch horses thunder down the track."

It didn't take long for me to alert my intuitive side on the drive there. I looked for signs. Not road signs, but sometimes I'd see a number that kept popping into my view or a name or something that was a clue for me to bet on a particular horse. It probably was dumb, so I never mentioned it to Angelo or anyone else. Sometimes I dreamed of a number and had to figure out how to play it or which race to bet. This wasn't science but long shots did come in, as did first-time-out jockeys.

I didn't win often, but it did happen. On those days I felt dead-right-certain about the bet I planned to make. Still my bet wasn't more than $2. I absolutely knew that if I bet more, which spelled *greedy* to me, I wouldn't win. I was happy with my $2 bets and even happier when it worked!

The first stop after we arrived was the hot dog stand. They were the best! It was like some people had to eat popcorn when they went to the movies. With us, it was the track hot dogs no matter which track. Mine, with kraut and mustard. Ah, they tasted even better than when I was a kid! Angelo liked his plain. I never saw him eat sauerkraut until years later when I cooked it at home; rinsed the vinegar off and heated it with olive oil. He loved it! I'd never find it on an Italian menu, though. My German ancestors were probably turning in their graves.

At first I mostly watched how things worked. I watched people, too. The track had lots of characters easy to read, describe or sketch. I just watched them. Sometimes we left our seats and went trackside to the rail to watch the horses parade out to the track with their escort ponies. They warmed up a bit jogging easily on the track until it was time to step into the starting gate. It took a few moments for all the horses to get in the gate. This was often an antsy few minutes.

Some horses hesitated and didn't want to go in the narrow space. I could feel the tenseness of the crowd, almost like they were holding their breath, after all they had money laid down. Then the gates popped open, everyone let go of that tension and they tensed their muscles, mentally running with the horses. The were off and moving fast! Daily race forms and newspapers were rolled up into fists!

For a few minutes the race crowd carried a tense quiet, holding tight until the horses got about half way round the track. The crowd loosened! Yelling began at that moment. It was like a maestro of the orchestra with a baton giving the signal *you can all start shouting now*. The screams of jockeys' names, horses' names, anything at all. *C'mon, baby! You can do it! Come on!!* Arms raised, hands in the air wrapped around rolled up racing forms, flapping in the breeze. People actually jumped up and down! The noise of the crowd rose higher like the orchestra when the creshendo reached its peak!

The winnng horse crossed the finish line! A second and third followed. The winning crush of people were ecstatic with hoorays as most were let-down, releasing moans, groans, sometimes curses, accusations against the jockey, horse or trainer. The losing tickets dropped onto the ground blowing here and there. Some tore them before tossing them up in the air.

The routine would start all over again for the next race. It was a hoot to watch!

Angelo's friend and horse track buddy Vic, teased me about betting on Julie Krone because she was a female. I knew he was impressed by her riding, too. She was usually the only female jockey racing in the daily form at the time. That too, would change.

It didn't take me long to become a super-fan of hers. Female jockeys could no longer be denied their place on the track. Only a few rode but more were trickling into the racing scene one by one. Julie took a lot of abuse; especially some guys (foul-mouthed pigs) at the rail who shouted loud sexual remarks to her. She ignored them, but I knew she heard them. I wondered if they thought they flustered her and kept her from riding her best. They didn't. She *always* gave her best. It showed in the awards and prestige she quickly gained.

At this time, she started to make her mark. I believed in her abilities and pocketed some coins from her races. It was exciting to go down to the paddock and watch her seat the horse, always easy to smile, crop in hand, cap in place and pairs of goggles ready to drop over her eyes. (I overheard that one pair of goggles were tossed when they became too muddy to see through, leaving the clean pair underneath to finish the race.)

I wondered if or how much grief she had to take breaking into the all-boys' club of horse racing. I read later that she and Mike Smith (a top jockey) were close friends over the racing years. I was glad some decent male jockeys were not threatened by her talent and tenacity.

In time, Julie Krone broke bones, healed, and put a leg up again. I liked her spunk and determination. Knowing how hard it was in those days for a woman to enter a previously man's field made me extra supportive. I looked for her mounts and was disappointed when she was out, but knew she healing from one injury or another.

Her later record showed that she was the only woman to ever win the Triple Crown and she did it in 1993 up on Colonial Affair! In time, she became the leading jockey, male or female, on *four* different race tracks. She retired from racing in 2004 after becoming a member of the National Women's Hall of Fame, National Cowgirl Hall of Fame, and the Michigan Sports Hall of Fame.

Chapter 3
Freehold Raceway
Freehold, New Jersey

I *had* been to a racetrack once before I met Angelo on the urging of a customer, a groom. I was tending bar in the pre-1850 American House, an historical country tavern restaurant that relied on the many horse farms in the New Egypt area for its' income. All associated with feeding, training and racing horses came into the tavern, walkers, grooms, trainers, jockeys, owners, and those that cheered their favorite horse to the finish line. They were a friendly lot. I listened to their stories, complaints, joys and dreams.

Photos of winning horses, standardbreds mostly, trotters and pacers; some rhoroughbreds, lined the walls of the tavern and restaurant. Their owners and trainers stood proudly alongside their winning horse. Horse racing paraphernalia hung on the walls and from ceiling beams. This was a new world to me. I did more listening about this *Sport of Kings* than anything else. I liked who these people were and appreciated how hard they worked, dedicated to the animals that needed and demanded attention every day, every week, all year long including holidays. The weather never kept them from the job or whatever took the average person indoors.

One afternoon, a couple of us from the tavern went to Freehold Raceway. It was a small country track then, sparsely attended during the week. A scattering of people sat in the grandstand or stood along the fence.

I knew absolutely zilch about racing but bet $2 on a tip given to me by the groom. Yep, the horse ran last. "Oh, well." I was there, did it and was satisfied this was not for me. My losing ticket slipped into my jeans pocket and waited for the next race to begin. We stayed for another losing race and left.

Roger, our resident handyman could fix just about anything in the building. We worked together for months before a customer revealed to me that Roger was once a top winning thoroughbred jockey!

He probably could still qualify by weight and height, but those years were far behind him. He was about 5' tall, wiry slender, with a huge handlebar mustache that kept him from being blown away in a storm. He was very proud of it and was a good guy in my book. We shared a lot of stories and opinions but he never talked about himself. I was sure he was Canadian, and itching to know, yet thought it best to honor his privacy.

Most of the area farms trained standardbreds. These were trotters and pacers that raced pulling a two-wheeled cart called a sulky. The training was quite different from thoroughbreds.

The sound of sulkies coming up the track was cool. It's very distinctive. A driver must have a sensitive talent to keep his cart wheels from catching the wheels of any other. Accidents were devastating.

The betting itch never got under my skin for good reason. I clearly remembered watching my mother, who loved racing and any form of gambling except cards, get into hot water when I was in high school. It made an impression on me.

Mom loved excitement. She had several years of tough life keeping my two brothers and me together when my father went into the hospital with an undiagnosed disease that would keep him there for seven years before he passed away. Mom was uneducated and had never worked outside the home.

Her father was a gentleman in the sense that he was raised without having the concern of earning money, until the crash of '29 anyway. He and my grandmother Elizabeth (Betty) traveled in high style visiting horse racing tracks and casinos around the country back in the heyday. Mom, an only child, was left at home with the nanny. It was not unusual for her dad Harry, to come in after midnight, still in tuxedo and top hat. Her mom in elbow length gloves and diamond tiara, woke their young daughter up, cover her and the bed with all the money he won that evening. No wonder Mom liked the high life. Unfortunately, her finances could not sustain such a lifestyle.

When she bet with the bookies, didn't win, didn't have the money, and didn't have a job to get the money, she broke into a sweat. She'd heard how bookies collect their money when it wasn't brought to them. This was New Jersey with lots of *intimidation* close at hand. Since she valued her kneecaps, she went to her fiancé Joe and pleaded with him to make her an honest woman, not by marrying, but by paying her bookie.

Bless the man. He did.

The second time it happened, he said "go to work or get a pair of crutches."

He stayed away for a week. My brother Bobby and I had no idea what was going on but we were rooting for Joe. We weren't a hugging-type family but accepted and was happy to have Joe included as part of our family.

Eventually, after much pleading on her part, he *loaned* her the money with a final warning. No more. Period.

Joe acted the role of our stepfather, without moving into our house, taking on *head of household* responsibilities without benefit of hearth and home. He

25

came for supper every night then took the bus to his family home. He made a tremendous difference in our lifestyle and treated Mom with the greatest respect while making her life better and easier. She would not marry him or allow him to move in until we kids were adults on our own.

I insisted he walk me down the aisle (Mom thought it was proper for my oldest brother to take my father's place. Even then I was not about being proper.) when my storybook wedding, which Joe paid for, took place. I spoofed propriety; never thought highly of being proper. They moved to Florida two years later and lived happily for ten years and married before he became ill and passed away.

Our trip to Yonkers was a one-time visit; a kind of introduction to Angelo's world. Philadelphia Park and Freehold were closer to home for weekly visits. Every track had its months during the year for meets. Being *dark*, meant they were not licensed to meet until a later time scheduled.

This was the groundwork for my introduction to the racing life as long as I was by Angelo's side.

With the memory of my mother's experience stuck in the back of my head, I continued being a $2 bettor per race. My limit of ten dollars for the day was enough to enjoy a full afternoon of excitement. Well, excitement when I won and even when I didn't really. I could cheer for a jockey I liked even if I didn't have money on the race.

The history of any place where I spent time interested me. Eventually I learned racing was held at the Freehold location since the 1830s. Racing didn't stop during the War Between the States. Instead a world record was set in 1863 by the *Pride of Monmouth County*, George M. Patchen, reported as trotting-under-saddle with a two-mile mark of 4:56. The horse was 14 years old!

Chapter 4
More Freehold
Harness Racing

Knowledge that I did bring to our outings and Angelo shared with me, was a love of good Italian food, including being picky about pizza. We definitely were pizza snobs. I still am today. Good pizza or the Italian Tomato Pie of my youth growing up on the border of Chambersburg, the Italian section of Trenton, is hard to find today. Everything changes.

Our next trip to Freehold Raceway found us driving east when the day of racing ended, instead of driving into the setting sun to come home. We found this welcoming place, away from the bitterly cold, open field winds of Freehold Raceway when one of Angelo's customers strongly suggested that we try Federici's Restaurant on E. Main St. in downtown Freehold. It was the beginning of a long-time love affair with Federici's food and family.

The loving aroma of olive oil, garlic and tomatoes simmering in the air greeted us at the door. Ah. We walked in from the Main street entrance the first time. (The next time and foerever after, we entered from the rear door entrance in the parking lot.) The front door brought us into a taproom with the bar on the right where a friendly bartender greeted us with a "Welcome folks, c'mon in!"

We waded through, passing tables on the left, to enter the warmth of the dining room. Low-backed upholstered banquet seats lined the right side with small tables that could be pushed together if needed. Larger, family-sized tables were on the left cozied in by an overhang that I suspect were closed-in stairs going to the second floor.

The table arrangements encouraged conversation with strangers. Angelo loved that! He was a social man who loved to talk to people. Most of the time they talked back, if not, he left them to their privacy.

We started by ordering the best thin crust pizza we ever ate, ever, taken with a glass or two of good, Italian red table wine. Soon other nights of the week found us driving to Federici's to savor their pizza without going to the races. Other items on the menu began to tease our taste buds. Trying out their menu became a test ground. Eggplant Parmegiana, always a favorite of mine and a test of a restaurant chef's ability to do it right by frying eggplant slices individually, before putting them in the casserole, made a big difference in the meal. I was delighted at Federici's!

Because we habitually went on the same nights of the week, we came to know our waiter, who later became a daughter-in-law of the owners. She fitted into the family restaurant plan perfectly! There was always a warm greeting from her each time we arrived. Sometimes she'd sneak us in ahead of someone else waiting, leading us to her station.

When Angelo suffered a serious bout with his heart, we didn't get to Federici's for several weeks. She noticed, mentioned missing us and took time to listen, truly interested in Angelo's health problem.

Family news was offered; who was in love, getting married, having babies, vacation plans, etc. She quietly, almost whispered, about her and her husband's dream of opening a satellite Federici's. They eventually did.

Frank, son of the original owners, Frank and Esther, and known as Spat often came to our table to chat. He and Angelo naturally discussed horses with great enthusiasm. Later, inklings filtered down that Spat was also a horse owner.

It felt like we were going to grandma's house for dinner when we stepped over the threshold at Federici's. We lamented when they closed for renovations and rejoiced over the new look when they reopened.

Reading the family history on the menu and listening to talk, we learned how their parents opened as Frank's Beer Garden in 1921, grew to Frank's Bar & Grill and finally to Federici's with the third generation being a big part of the business. Later, the fourth generation added to their success. They kept expanding, changing, growing as they needed to do because there was usually a line of people waiting for a table if we didn't get there early enough. And we went earlier and earlier so we wouldn't have to wait.

Even Bruce Springsteen, born and raised in Freehold, managed to come back to Federici's when he wanted good pizza. It's been noted that he liked pepperoni on his with some cold beer to wash it down.

A devastating fire at Freehold Raceway in early May of '84 destroyed the grandstand and the dining room area. The fire began from an electrical short somewhere near the tote board in a brick building at 6:30 a.m.

Easter Morn won in the last race the day before. Amazingly, more than 600 horses onsite were evacuated without being harmed, nor were any people injured. Another 500 horses usually stabled at the track were displaced. Three hundred employees lost their jobs overnight and some had never worked elsewhere.

By then I was going to the track with Angelo every Monday. We saw the aftermath of the fire. It was sad and disheartening to see such catastrophie. But racing continued. The winter meet that year was tough. Winds swept across the vast open fields like blasts from the North Pole. They chilled my bones and whipped my hair into a wild mop while going from the tent erected for the temporary betting cages to place a bet, to the fence to watch the race. The tent stopped the wind but the cold rose from the ashphalt working its way into my bones. Brr.

The lack of an enclosed grandstand didn't slow down the sport. Racing went on as usual. The fans had cold hands clutching the daily race forms. A few even wore hats and scarves. It takes more than being frozen half to death to deter a race fan. I looked around (being a people–watcher) and saw the same intensity on their faces, only the faces were red from low, frigid temperatures and high winds.

Our interest drifted from Freehold Raceway to other places during the rebuilding and we returned to the track only once after it was completed..

Chapter 5
Plaza de Toros
Cancun, Mexico

Our visit began with a shocking surprise! The hotel on the beach was artfully designed, enhanced with brilliant, lush, tropical flowers and palm trees. The ground level with the check-in counter and lobby area was completely open with no walls at all! Tables covered in white linen filled one area while gentle breezes swept through, waiting for the dining hour. Fat, round columns supported the upper levels. We dragged our luggage to the first upper floor, whipped out our room key and entered . . . to find a couple with their arms clinging to each other, humping away in the middle of our king-size bed!

Stunned and embarrassed that we interrupted honeymooners, I checked the room key. The number was correct. It took a minute until I realized they weren't guests in the wrong room, we weren't in the wrong room, they were employees sneaking a quickie! We retreated to the desk downstairs and, without much comment, given a different room overlooking the beautiful, turquoise Caribbean Sea.

At first I was annoyed but then thought, *what the heck I have no idea what their lives are like, what their needs are, only that they are taking a chance to release a little passion. Who am I to judge?*

I laughed to myself and recalled that I read *Don't Stop the Carnival!* by Herman Wouk 30 years ago and still remember the same scene in his book!

I wasn't overly happy with Angelo's choice of Cancun for a vacation even though we were here the first week in January. It was icy cold back in Jersey and it was hot and sunny here. How ungrateful could I be? But exploring new territory was my style for a trip away. I didn't connect exploring with this

Cancun. It struck me as a place to flip a towel on the beach and lay on it. Angelo liked the sun on his face and could sit or lay under the sun for hours. So, after a December that was overwork for both of us, me with a gift shop to run and Angelo super busy because everyone wanted a fresh haircut for the holiday.

After settling in to our new room, we spent the rest of the afternoon in the fancy swimming pool that was designed with an island in the middle to table our drinks in between swims. How pleasantly a swim and a cocktail relaxed me. We dipped into the Caribbean Sea first but I refused to just lie on the beach. Boring.

A life-size Nativity Scene was displayed between the hotel and the beach. The roof and sides were thatched. At night a couple guitar players strummed and sang Christmas songs. No one else was around. Angelo jumped right in and talked the guy with the guitar to let him try it. Laughing, I took pictures. No one at home would believe it otherwise. I was certain the guitarist wouldn't forget it either.

Our travel agent *strongly* advised against renting a car in Mexico. "Tourists in cars run into big problems in Mexico. There are many unsafe places away from your resort area. It is as if they spot an easy set-up to make money on false claims, accidents, etc. Besides that, a bus into town runs passed your hotel every 10 minutes." I followed her advice but it was another reason for me to grumble about Cancun.

The bus did come by that quickly and we took it to the small town nearby, found a charming outdoor restaurant with lots of thatch for the roof and low walls. I think to mark off territory. It didn't seem like a permanent building. It was a great location to people-watch both in the restaurant and walking by. Angelo chose Cabrito, goat stew and I went for

34

the fish. Yummy. Things were looking up. We were both pleased. After dinner we walked to an open-air café around the corner where a guitarist was playing. Over expresso coffees Angelo promised the owner, who had come over to chat with us, that we would be back the following night for dinner. We did.

It was a good promise to keep. Angelo ordered Risotto with caramelized radicchio and I got to taste the Cabrito I missed the night before. It was a delicate flavor, not heavy at all. Probably could be compared to white meat chicken, but tastier. The chilled white wine was excellent and reasonable in price. Everything was perfect. The murmur of voices happy to be here floated through the room with the notes of the musicians playing at a soft tempo for dinner time. We sauntered through the street, me looking for interesting items to take back to my shop to resell. Angelo found someone to ask about directions and procedure to the ruins. So, we would be exploring after all!

We arranged a visit to Plaza de Toros. The bullfights were the heart of Mexico and only held once a week. A sparsely occupied bus picked us up at the hotel and drove directly to the location. I was Cliente #18950.

The sun was high and the grandstand that circled around the arena was only 1/4 full with people scattered around. While we waited in the grandstands Angelo struck up a conversation with a group sitting near us. They were chatting about the ruins they visited the day before. He was happy to hear their comments about it, planting the idea for us to see what they talked about.

Mariachi music blared out as a parade of people skipped into the arena. Charros dressed in their typical tight pants with bright embroidery, flared at the cuff, ruffled shirts, short jackets, and sporting large sombreros, performed first bringing happy sounds and gaity to the moment.

Next, representing the national dance of Mexican folklore, a man and woman performed the Mexican Hat Dance. It told the story of a man pursuing the woman he loved after having his marriage proposal refused. He persisted. She finally accepted him as the dance ended. They wore brilliant costumes; he similar to the charro, she in a floor length, multi-ruffled dress that flounced and flared as she twisted and turned. This was more like the Mexico I read about.

Finally a bugle announced the bull and the matador were entering the bullring. He looked elegant in his exquisite *suit of lights* as he walked proudly into the bullring ready to do battle with the bull. He truly took his life in his hands. The bull was a frightening size!

Back in 1968 I read *Or I'll Dress You in Mourning,* a biography written by Larry Collins. It was the magnetic story of El Cordobes who was a dirt poor boy who survived learning to be a bullfighter, to become a millionaire. It didn't come easily. This was the 1990s and my mind still carried his struggle, pain and sorrow. Remembering his eventual fame glowed within me. I could feel El Cordobes' pride as this matador stepped into the ring. Goosebumps popped up on my arms, as excitement burst out.

After a few minutes of the bullfight, already tense with the dance of daring between bull and man, Angelo, as the gentle man he was, started to squirm. "Let's go," he said. "I don't like this."

I took my eyes off the bull and matador to look at him. "No way," I replied. "Turn away or go for a walk." That was it. No one could tear me away from seeing this live, even though we were pretty high up in the bleachers.

It wasn't seeing the bull hurt, dying even. It was the whole history of bullfighting, of toreros and their bravery in facing a bull that weighed 900 to 1500 pounds charging at him. Many bullfighters have died from being in the ring (as boxers do in our country). It was the essence of the Spanish peoples. That was the thrill for me, it's why I ate Cabrito, to taste the Spanish/Mexican way of life. We stayed.

The matador whipped his cape around daring the bull to charge. The bull, after he scraped the ground with his hoof, charged the matador and missed him. The challenge came again and again. They went back and forth. Finally the matador walked away. The announcer explained that because the bull was brave, the matador released him and allowed the bull to live. I was happy. I saw the dance of the matador and the bull. No one was hurt in the process. I was happy that the bull was not killed. Angelo was quiet and relieved, too.

Two days before we were to leave, we took the regular bus into town, fought our way through the crowds and found the bus station. Instead of taking a pre-arranged tour, we stepped onto a different bus along with the people who lived and worked here. We got on the bus to see the way of life of the Mexican people, not other tourists. Not an English speaker among them; all chattered away in Spanish not paying any attention to two obvious gringos. They carried their lunches, cages of chickens, bundles, bags overflowing, dragging children and baskets of fruit on their heads. This was serious business. I watched out the window, soaking up the true life lived here.

In one village was a glaring, white, 6' high wall gleaming in the now, high sun. All along the top of the wall were sparkling (from the brilliant sun) broken bottles, glass shards, spikey chunks of glass, all of different colors, sizes, shapes, points upward. At first I thought, *artistically how beautiful this was*, until I realized it was to keep people out, to hurt them if they climbed it. It told me a lot about the neighborhood. Apparently not a safe one even though it looked very nice. Clean, it was a neat neighborhood.

In a couple hours we arrived at Tulum, stepped off the bus with a few other riders. There was nothing in sight except a small, charming looking one-room hacienda with a fenced in patio lush with flowers and greenery. A sign said *restaurant.* Angelo said, "Let's stop and eat first."

He surprised me. "Not a good idea. Remember where we are."

The place was comfy, snug. A place a tourist could trust? Angelo ordered Polzole de Guajolote, a wild turkey stew. I caved and ordered a small salad just so I wasn't staring at him while he ate.

I was sipping my bottled water a little at a time. *Don't Drink the Water!* had been said to me each time I mentioned we were going to Mexico. I had not imbibed a drop of tap water anywhere. Now we were in the middle of nowhere, in the hot, hot afternoon with glaring sun burning into me. I was a girl born to wear boots and sweaters. What was I doing here?

There were no signs, so when Angelo finished eating we walked in the direction the other people went. In the middle of nowhere, there was a small table, one chair and the man sitting there was collecting money to visit the ruins. No pamphlets were offered. No maps were seen. It was all open, no gate or fence or anything surrounding the area to keep you out if you didn't pay.

Finally we saw some folks up ahead and approached what once was the walled city of Tulum. It was a Mayan seaport hub built high on the edge of rocky cliffs, overlooking the gorgeous white caps on turquoise water of the Caribbean. White sands lay at the bottom of the cliffs. Not a soul was on the beach. Tulum was famous for its turquoise and jade that brought major world trade to their port in the 13th to the 15ᵗʰ centuries before the Spanish came and conquered.

At this time it was rocks tumbled every-where. A few structures were off in the distance. We came upon what looked like a temple, still standing atop many crumbling, uneven steps. I was dragging from one area to another, tried not to complain, totally miserable from the sun beating down, heat and running out of water. We did this all wrong which made it unbearable for me to appreciate. We didn't have enough water and I really needed a hat that I didn't have. The sun energized Angelo. He moved around like he was in his own backyard, making comments to strangers and loving every minute. I was a rag.

It was a long day but we made it back to the hotel just before *Montezuma's Revenge* hit me! Diarrhea! Stomach cramps! I had been so careful on this trip but weakened over that wee bit of salad. What was I thinking??? I now drank bottle after bottle of water trying to flush this out of my system. I stayed in my room all the next day and the day after we were leaving. Thankfully. Angelo, who ate hot, cooked food at the hacienda, was fine.

This was travel where pre-planning on my part would have worked better..

Chapter 6
Monmouth Park
Oceanport, New Jersey

On Sunday afternoons in the summer, we took the hour-long drive to one of my favorite racetracks. This one was in Monmouth Park, Oceanport (NJ). The drive from Bordentown where we bought an old, Victorian apartment house to live in, went north on Rte. 130 to Rte. 33 east, through Freehold and Colt's Neck passing some elegant horse farms. We came home the same way so we could continue to stop at our favorite Federici's.

This track was originally built in the 1870s as a tourist attraction to aid the Jersey Shore crowds. Its high caliber of horses dubbed it *The Newmarket of America* hinting at the famous racecourse in England. Yet, in three years the Park had financial difficulties and closed.

When Amory L. Haskell reopened the Park in 1946, he lobbied to make parimutuel betting legal for thoroughbreds and standardbreds. His excellent leadership kept Monmouth Park the classy affair it started out to be in the previous century. That's what I saw when we started going there. The historical feel of those bygone days was one of the things I loved about this track! The race meet lasted from Opening Day in May into September.

An abundance of flowers overflowed everywhere, in window boxes, in huge pots scattered throughout the grounds, greeting everyone at the entrances. The macadum was clean of litter, except for a few losing tickets. The Park was shiny with fresh paint each year, gleaming white rail fences around the oval and paddock area. The outdoor concession stands were painted in Monmouth Park Kelly Green. They were kept immaculate and offered Deli sandwiches of fresh cold cuts, hoagies, and other items besides hot dogs. The Deli gazebo was always painted a brilliant white.

Picnic tables shaded by matching green and white striped umbrellas were off to the side for family outings . Children had plenty of room to run around safely while their parents watched the horses run. It was summertime and the Park wanted everyone to enjoy their visit and come back again.

The focus was placed on special racing days with added amusements, such as Mother's Day, Annual Irish Festival, Father's Day, Wine & Chocolate Fest, Italian Festival, BBQ & Craft Beer Fest, Classic Car Show & Oldies Day, Tu Sello Latino Day, etc. Giveaways were featured on those and other particular days.

The design of Monmouth Park was so spacious that when the big crowds *did* come on special event days, it still wasn't overcrowded. The open-air grandstand was newly painted each year and sported flowerboxes brilliant with color even along the outside of the enclosed air conditioned area. All was kept fresh and clean.

Larger purses were offered, so I figured these were a better class horse than other local tracks. I learned by observation. I watched my favorite jockey Julie Krone win races, filling my pocket with small wins. The better rider she became, the fewer long shots happened.

Because I loved and enjoyed being at this track, my instinct heightened here. Maybe a bit of psychic ability plugged in now and then. I stayed loose and listened to the little bird whisper in my ear about who was going to win next.

Other jockeys familiar to me from Philadelphia Park also rode here. One talented rising star jockey Chris Antley. (During this period of the 1980s he was the first jockey to win 9 races on 9 different horses in one day at one track. Sadly he later struggled with drug addiction and was murdered in 2000 in his California home.) Also Lafitt Pincay, Jr., Jorge Velazquez, and Chris McCarron were on the Racing Form, too.

I enjoyed stepping into this other world by going down to the paddock to watch the trainers saddle the horses, put their hands together to give a leg up to the jockeys dressed in their vividly colored silks and walk the horses to the parade ring. The horses were brushed until they gleemed in the sun, sleek, anxious to run. I looked into their eyes as they paraded by, walking under the grandstand to the track. Then I went to the window to make a bet before sitting in the open air grandstand or sometimes standing at the rail.

These were lazy, warm, summer Sundays, the pace was slow, people were pleasantly enjoying themselves in the holiday picnic atmosphere. All was well in the world when we were at Monmouth Park.

A year after Angelo passed away in '96, one of the neighborhood teenage girls, Rebecca, came into the bookshop to chat as she often did. She asked if I would take her and her girlfriend to Monmouth Park. I did. After receiving permission from her guardian. (Her parents had passed away.) We spent a lovely day there. I placed a $2 bet for her, and fortunately for her, she lost. I was glad. I've seen too many people get hooked because of that first winning ticket that sucked them in to a lifetime of misery. Especially when they were young, impressionable, and looking for easy money. Of course we stopped at Federici's. It was a nostalgic day for me, one of peace and closure.

Chapter 7
Sudbury Downs
Sudbury, Ontario, Canada

Way before we could see Niagara Falls, the thundering rumble overtook every thought, filling me with excitement. Mile by mile, the intensity of the roar increased, louder and louder, generating my body to vibrate from sound! Unable to sit still, I itched to again see the origin formulating the drumming of a giant sending such a throbbing out into the atmosphere, even overpowering the sound of the radio.

We were travel-minded, curious about other countries, their cultures and their racetracks. One of our earliest escapades began in August 1985. It started out as a fishing trip. We drove north leaving New Jersey, going through Pennsylvania and New York, closing in on Canada.

I had been here before in dreary winter, still, hearing the rumble, expecting something spectyacular, and I knew the American side of the Falls fell short. It looked and felt industrial; all wires, steel, and business. We drove straight across the Niagara River.

Our passports were ready. No problems. It was as easy as stopping the car and saying hello to the officer on duty.

Seeing the Canadian Falls sent tremors through my body as I stood with mouth open, unable to absorb the immensity, the pounding of water, the spray on this hot, July, summer day, shooting up and over the edge to soak everything it reached. The gigantic power again stunned me to almost a shock. This beauty on a sunny day overwhelmed.

Nature was at its wildest, most violent, blotting out everything else!. It was nearly impossible to look at the surrounding area. I couldn't take my eyes away from the Falls.

Images of explorers 300 or more years ago went through my mind. What fears rose in them, before they reached the Falls, when they did not know what to expect from the thunderous noise that permiated everything for miles!

We tore ourselves away to explore the rest of the city of Niagara Falls with a drive-by. It was overflowing with an abundance of summer flowers bursting out of containers and gardens sending color everywhere. Thick, emerald green grass-filled islands in the road creating a complementary background for the flowers. It was a breath-taking spectacle.

No lingering for us because we had a distance to drive yet, nearly five hours due north to French River. Arriving in daylight was probably best. Our plan was to stay for three days. As we drove away from Niagara, the road became a two-lane road with much less traffic.

Hour after hour, we saw immense rock boulders, some-times towering over us, lining the road as we drove through them. The further north we traveled, the more plentiful they became, jutting out of the ground everywhere as if they popped up unexpectedly. The drive took us through areas looking more remote. Dense forests of pine trees lined the sides of the road.

I took note that when a car was traveling slower, the drivers would pull over to a space the first chance they could, to let the car behind go by. Spaces were sparse but I was impressed to see this courtesy. When I returned home I made it part of my driving habit. Many times a driver would look at me with an odd expression as if they were asking me, why? They just didn't get it in super crowded Jersey roads. I did it anyway.

Nearing our destination, we scanned the pine trees

looking for a big sign. No commercial signage littered this roadway at all. Finally we spotted a small sign, not more than a foot long and half that high, tucked into the trees. Sand Beach Lodge.

A dirt road wide enough for one car led us through the forest. No problem of running into another car, I didn't think there were any other cars within miles from here anyway. Pine trees and huge boulders filled in everywhere. They were probably left from the big ice age melt. I'm sure wild animals roamed freely which made me happy to be *inside* the car.

As we pulled into the clearing, hosts Dean and Erla Wenborne came out to greet us. They cheerfully led us to a picturesque log lodge overhanging the water. This charming place was the dining and social room.   Logs were the interior walls, too. Hanging Native Canadian wool blankets and hand crafted woven floor mats were the decor. It left lots of wood exposed to create a natural warmth and welcome. It oozed the charm of two centuries earlier. Comfort filled the air. I felt right at home.

Erla gave us general information and arranged for us to go out on the lake to fish the next day with a Native Canadian guide. .

Dean pointed to our log cabin off in the distance, surrounded by trees with a cleared space just wide enough to park the car. The lake was a stone's throw from the door. We drove over, parked, and stood absorbing the peace of place. It was as quiet as a church at 3 a.m., giving off the sense of holiness. Beautiful. Serene. Restorative.

We unpacked, settled in and went to the lodge for a hearty supper of fresh baked fish, mashed potatoes, stewed tomatoes, and warm rolls with butter. We talked for a while and called it a night.

It was just before 11 p.m.when we entered the cabin. I didn't bother to turn on the wall lamp. It was the end of summer when the sky stayed light late. As we prepared for bed, the darkness fell like a blackout curtain. It became so dark instantly that we couldn't see our own hands held up in front of our faces. We laughed at this oddity. I peeked out the door for just a second and it was even darker, if possible.

I closed the door and locked it tight. Hearing crackling sounds outside, we both wondered about the animals roaming around us, hoping no bears would try to get in. We left home in Jersey that morning at 5 a.m. I was beat. The tension of driving long distance always knocked me out.. I climbed into bed. In seconds, I was sound asleep, forgetting about bears, moose, cougars, or anything that might roam around.

The morning was early, bright, sunny, and cheerful. The clean, crisp air kicked up our appetites as we headed to the lodge for a hearty breakfast of ham, bacon, eggs, and home fries. Hot biscuits were served with butter and local honey.

Afterwards, Dean introduced us to Joe, our guide; a tall, big-boned, rugged man. A face that showed he preferred outdoors. He carried a woodsy appearance, full head of black hair with bits of gray, lean, muscled, sun-browned, and silent. Even his movements were quiet. A self-contained man.

Joe didn't say much, kind of just grunted a greeting as he led us to the boat. He wasn't abrasive, just not a talker or a man who used social skills. He loaded the gear while we climbed into the boat. Since fishing was something we did often at home, we brought our gear with us. Apparently different kind of poles, hooks, etc. were used here so we advisedly left our things in the cabin.

Off we went, headed out into the wilderness. It was peaceful, yet exhilarating! I felt like I could just reach up and pull down the puffy, white clouds that hung low above us. I thought it mightt be the altitude that made them appear so close. This was the most beautiful, pristine place that I ever visited. It could have been the year 1600. The air smelled pure. The water sparkled, clear and cold. Colors were vivid in sky and shoreline. A quiet lay naturally over the land. I think even Angelo felt it. He was quiet too, for a little while, anyway. Highly unusual for him.

Joe set up our poles, hooking bait on mine. I let him. Angelo did his own. Maybe that was a manly thing. We fished in a comfortable silence. I was overwhelmed with the beauty, purity of this day, place, knowing this moment would never come again. It was a one and only time. I felt as if I belonged here.

Serenity blessed the area. Good spirits were all around us, respectfully quiet for us to absorb, hold close, and keep forever.

I think the guide used some native juice to bless me with some luck. I caught a fish barely large enough to keep, although I didn't because what would I do with it? Angelo never got a bite. If his ego was bruised, he didn't say. Our guide caught a big fish, large enough for lunch for the three of us.

At high noon, he pulled the boat up to a huge rock outcrop and unloaded his pack. Silent as a crumb falling to the floor, he pulled out his cast iron fry pan, peeled the potatoes, onion, and breaded his caught fish after cleaning it, built a fire, heated a bit of something in the pan, and cooked everything to perfection. Aromas curled around tantalizing us while it was cooking. Breakfast had been digested long ago and fresh air whipped up a healthy appetite. A pot of coffee on an open fire was the period at the end of the sentence. It was the best meal ever!

Joe wouldn't let me help clean up. I didn't push it either, sensing it wasn't the right thing to do..

Angelo was a friendly talker. He talked to everyone. But he couldn't get a syllable out of the guide. The man wasn't rude. He was just a quiet man. One who could fish and cook!

Back in the gathering room at the main lodge at supper time, Angelo began a conversation with someone who *would* answer him. This other guest gave him directions to harness racing at Sudbury Downs near Chelmsford. It would take less than an hour to drive, if you were a local and knew the way. We went that night and stayed too late.

We found it easily enough. There weren't many roads to distract us or take us the wrong way. I think Angelo had a nose that followed a horse racing scent, finding a track like the old cowboy movies had Native American scouts who could find water.

Racing in such a faraway place was fun. The simple, country track conducted races two nights a week, Wednesday and Saturday. So we were lucky to be there on the right night. Maybe to make up for only two nights, they ran ten to fourteen races! Wow! That's a lot of racing in one visit!

The building was nothing fancy, a basic cinder block and glass with bleachers, no adornments, very basic and plain. The gift shop was a small corner near the entrance with one small glass counter. I bought a watch as a Christmas present for Angelo and tucked it into my bag. The face of it showed a horse, racing around from number to number. (At Christmas he really got a kick out of it, even though he never wore a watch. He showed it off to the guys in the barber shop.)

I only bet one race.. Watching people and their reactions was more fun. It was still light when we left after several races. The race night was not over yet for the locals, but they probably knew their way home in the dark.

The way back to the lodge was a two lane road cut through the forest of pine trees and hardwoods that reached high into the sky, trying to touch the stars. I was anxious and nervous about getting back to the lodge before dark. The dirt path entrance might be really hard to find.

Just as I feared, night came suddenly! Voom! Instant blackness! Everything was jet black except the small area that the highbeam headlights lit up! Fortunately, there were no other cars on the road so we crept along as we searched for that tiny, tiny Sand Beach Lodge sign. I was afraid we would have to ride up and down the road for miles trying to find that sign!

The sky behind us kept flaring up in beautiful colors. I glanced in the rear and side view mirrors but had no clue what was happening behind us. I *was* concerned and concentrating on what was in front of us. Thankfully no animals were about either. Later I learned the sky full of color was the Northern Lights.

Finally, we spotted the sign on our first run down the road. We slowly turned into the dirt track, creeping along, hoping no wild animals would approach the car. The cabin appeared without incident; a miracle in itself. I pulled right up to the cabin wall and left the headlights on until Angelo got into the cabin and turned the lights on for me. It was that dark! Stunning!

Chapter 8
Other New York City Area
Aqueduct Racetrack

Being among a New York City crowd gave the visit a completely different feeling. Everywhere was mobbed with people dropping enough losing tickets on the floor to make me sorry I didn't wear boots.

This crowd took pleasure in leaving a mess by tossing garbage on the floor, not just losing tickets. I tried to think positively and guessed it created jobs for some clean-up people. Maybe it was the attitude in the air that annoyed me. I did enjoy having a knish again. It was the first one I ate since Yonkers.

Belmont Park

I think Angelo just fueled his curiosity to see where the country's most famous horse racing events took place: the Triple Crown of Thoroughbred Racing. It consisted of three races for three year olds. Winning all three is the greatest accomplishment in thoroughbred racing in the USA.

The contest originated in 19th century England. The first step in the challenge was winning the Kentucky Derby's 1¼ mile dirt track race at Churchill Downs in Louisville, Kentucky. The second challenge was winning: the Preakness Stakes 1 1/16 mile dirt track race at Pimlico Race Course in Baltimore, Maryland. The third and final step was winning: the Belmont Stakes 1 ½ mile run on the dirt track in Elmont, New York.

It's probably safe to say the entire horse racing world watched the third leg of the Triple Crown whether they saw the first two or not. There were special parties, closed circuit TV and whatever else was available in the world. Belmont Park would be packed with racing fans from all over.

Racing's greatest legends, from Man O'War to Seabiscuit to Cigar ran here to the thrill and roar of more than New York crowds.

Belmont, sometimes called the Championship Track because so many of the major champion horses have competed here. It was considered an elite racetrack in the *Sport of Kings* as were Saratoga Race Course, Churchill Downs, Del Mar, and Santa Anita.

The grand opening of Belmont Park on May 4, 1905 attracted more than 40,000 fans who witnessed August Belmont II's Blandy, at 7-1 odds, hold off 100-1 long shot Oliver Cromwell in the $1,500 Belmont Inaugural.

Not to break a good habit, I thoroughly enjoyed a knish. For some reason I didn't have any winning luck at the New York City area tracks.

Chapter 9
CharlesTown
Charles Town, West Virginia

Angelo said he had an early Monday morning appointment, so we left early on Sunday morning and drove 3½ hours from New Jersey to Charles Town, West Virginia to go to the horse races. After the races we drove 3½ hours home again, stopping for dinner along the way. Whew! That was pure crazy.

It was another year before we went back to Charles Town. At my request, we first drove to Harper's Ferry at the confluence of the Shenandoah and Potomac Rivers. This side trip was to feed my history curiosity. I wanted to see the place I read about with such interest. Truly, reading sent me to many places I would not otherwise have desired to see.

Angelo sat in the car with a glass of our homemade wine accompanied by a slice of good bread coupled with Butirro cheese. He was quite content to let me wander alone so I could get a deep feeling of the site that held such violence and such a warning.

The river was rolling along in a lazy fashion on a pleasantly warm, sunny day. No rush. No reason to get excited. It was a rural setting, with a few Colonial-dated houses built going up a hill looking like they were going down a staircase sideways. No one else was around, only the quiet, the peacefulness, and me.

I thought that moment probably was not very different from the day before the explosive situation with abolitionist John Brown. He believed in his desperate attempt to arm and free all the slaves of the South with his small band of men. Armed slaves were the greatest fear that struck panic in the hearts of every plantation owner in the

South, and many who were not plantation owners!
Southerners drove some by extreme measures to assure that
it did not happen.

Foolish thinking on all sides. At least he opened the
moral issue. It spread far and wide.

I had no idea Charles Town was so close to the track. All we
saw were open fields. Later, regret set in for not checking a
map first, when I realized how close we were to the town.
With my love of history, I would have enjoyed seeing it.

We also would have found a nicer place to stay. We reserved
a really cheap motel room nearby to the track which looked
like stable hands stayed there, the ones who forgot their
mother's teachings about respect of other people's property.
It was shabby with cigarette burn holes on the tables and
chairs, but clean. I was praying no bedbugs would appear. It
was the only place available that we could find. We didn't
even see any place to get a bite to eat. There was nothing
around but fields.

Harness horse racing didn't impress me here. Perhaps the
mood had been set by my visit to Harper's Ferry. Maybe
after being to my favorite tracks, Monmouth Park and
Delaware Park; grand, gracious elder ladies as I thought of
them, spoiled me for other tracks and I hadn't even gone to
Saratoga Springs yet.

Angelo enjoyed it. But, then he always relaxed at the
races. Amazing.

We went to the Greyhound races that night. I read the
program and sticking to my commitment made two $2 bets,
this time without enthusiasm.

I tore up my losing tickets and just watched everyone else. The dog track did not interest me at all. I was unsettled. No idea why. Don't know if it was the history of Harper's Ferry or if the negative articles I read about dogs racing affected me. Still don't. I do know there is no sense in placing any bets when my mind is engaged in some kind of turmoil.

With my enthusiasm in supporting females saddled up, I must mention this other important historical fact that happened near Harper's Ferry, West Virginia. It was at the W. Virginia races in 1969 that Barbara Jo Ruben became the first female jockey to win a pari-mutual race in the United States. It was also the first track in the Northeast to offer winter racing.

Chapter 10
The Annual Horse Race
Australia, Part 1

At the stopover in the Hawaii airport, four Hawaiians greeted us as we alighted from the plane, stepping into a small lobby area to say *aloha*. Two men were playing ukuleles; two women were performing the hula dance. Since we were the last to come off the plane, we got to watch them scoot around the corner, drop their grass skirts, remove their leis, roll their jeans down and they were off and running! Extra money made for the day.

"Authentic" I said to Angelo with a wry smile.

There was a brief layover in Hawaii, not long enough for us to venture out of the airport to do any exploring. We flew from Jersey to California, boarded Qantas airlines for Hawaii and now waited to cross over the equator to land in Cairns, Queensland, Northeast Australia.

On arrival in Cairns at 8 a.m. we quickly found that our overnight case with the toiletries in it that I packed so carefully to have handy, did not arrive with us! This was disastrous! There was no place to freshen-up since we left Jersey a day and a half ago! To make matters worse it was much too early for us to check into our hotel. Smelling ripe was putting it mildly. Looking forward to a shower was putting it mildly too.

It was also a lesson in my psychic awareness. My tarot card reader told me we would be taking a trip over the ocean.

She also said, "One of your pieces of luggage will be lost, but don't worry. It will be returned to you later that night."

So, I didn't fuss, even though that was the reason I packed toiletries separate. When we boarded Qantas I was told the carryon was an inch too long. An inch! Oh, well. How ironic. Apparently some experiences cannot be avoided. However, I *was* concerned about body odor.

The receptionist was sympathetic, probably being able to smell us from the other side of the counter. He did allow us to leave our luggage behind the counter so we could stroll around the beautiful, flower laden, tropical town. Off we went to walk around the park, which seemed to be the center of town. We gratefully inhaled the glorious scent of lush flowers since our odor was the opposite.

Qantas fed us a full breakfast on the plane but without much else to do, we crossed the street to a little coffee shop. It was busy with people who came in for 'take-away' coffee and pastries on their way to work. A few ordered and sat down. It was Saturday, the busiest day of the week for retail.

There was always room for lattes so we relaxed, sipped, and nibbled warm, crisp croissants. As we were making small talk between us, a fellow leaned across the narrow aisle to our little table and spoke with enthusiasm.

"Americans, are you?"

"Yes," I said, smiling. "How could you tell?"

"Oh. I have friends from the States. I heard your accent right away. Is there anything I can help you with?"

Again I smiled. Angelo being born and raised in Italy still had a strong accent that was not American, unless this gent watched some of the old New Jersey movies.

Angelo immediately spoke up. "Are there any horse-racing tracks around?"

Magic words! Angelo always pops out with magic words! Our new friend Bob jumped right in with glee.

"The Annual Horse Race is scheduled for today at the fairgrounds. It is the biggest fund raiser of the year! The mayor and all the bigwigs, including the owners of the TV and radio stations, will be there under the Foster's Lager tent. That's the most popular beer in the country. Australians love their beer."

He continued to tell us that he owned a carpet shop around the corner. He seemed to be pondering.

"No one's going to come in today for carpet, because they're all going to be at the fairgrounds. Be ready at 11:30. I'll pick you up at your hotel and take you there."

As an afterthought, he said, "My wife will be mad, but she'll get over it and be glad again. In time."

I had to laugh at his comment. It must be a good marriage to be so sure of his wife.

Angelo's face lit up with joy! I was concerned with our scent. If we were going to hobnob with the bigwigs, we'd better smell nicer.

We bought a few items at the drug store that I tossed into my large tote bag. At least we got a chance to wash and freshen ourselves in the immaculate public restroom at the hotel. If we couldn't change our clothes at least we smelled better. Angelo bought a throw away razor and looked better, too.

As he promised, Bob picked us up, two strangers, at the hotel on time.

He drove giving us local information, talked about his son's tour guide business and gave us the young man's card.

We were off on an adventure; too busy talking to pay attention to how we were getting to where we were going. Bob drove like a wild teenager, fast, like someone may take his car away from him. We soon left the blacktopped roadway, zipped across open fields, bounced along, until we saw festive tents and flags flying high appearing on the horizon. Dust rose, leaving a trail behind us. He parked among the other cars and trucks.

It was as if we were prized treasures. Bob led us into the huge, white Foster's Lager tent filled with tables covered in white cloth, some were the larger round tables. All were filled with enthused people already in a party mood. Bob took us from table to table, introduced us to everyone, including the owners of the radio station, TV station, the Mayor, etc. etc. giving our New Jersey origin. He was enjoying this even more than we were.

This was a fancy crowd. Many of the guys were in suits with shirt and tie. As the sun heated the day, they began to open the top buttons, loosen their ties, and soon many removed their jackets to hang over the back of the chairs.

The ladies were dressed to the nines, like Kentucky Derby day in the States. All the women sported fancy hats, some big ones, all looking as if one was trying to outdo the next. No woman was without a hat of some kind, except me, and the Foster girls. They wore jockey caps and were dressed in brightly colored blue and white Foster silks, to give the jockeys competition in appearance. They joyfully played the role of bartenders and waiters for the day.

All were welcoming and jolly. A small town feeling of connectivity and camaraderie filled the tent. The more beer flowed, the louder it got.

Many men looked attractive as they sported white straw Panama hats. Later in the day, in fun, one tried to climb on stage with the ladies during the contest of the prettiest hat. No luck. He wasn't allowed among the dozen competing women. Laugher surrounded us.

Everyone was out to have a grand time. They were good at it. Voices and frosty mugs of beer were raised in good cheer, toasting whatever some creative mind could come up with.

After smiling until my face hurt and doing my bit to be a good American ambassador, I wandered outside, on my own, to see how the bookies worked *down under*.

There were several standing along the track railing. Each had a pole with paper squares of numbers attached to it. They each also had a blackboard standing nearby that they marked their odds on. The odds changed several times as people placed bets before the race began. I bet with whatever one had the odds I preferred. I could bet $2 each race or bet more. This was so cool, just like in the British movies I watched.

There were no stables that I could see or paddock or parade ring since this wasn't a professional track. It was just an open field that the fund raising committee commandeered. Eventually the horses came sauntering onto the track. The jockeys and horses were all amateurs as far as I knew. (Many years later I learned that this was a 3-day Carnival event that grew into professional racing.)

The crowd erupted as soon as the horses leapt ahead. As the horses ran the oval track that had been plowed, people yelled for their horse to win. Arms flailed and fists held winning betting slips and lots of losing ones. Horse hooves pounded on the makeshift track kicking up more dust in the air. It matched the excitement all around me.

The horses thundered around the fourth quarter to the home stretch, heading for the finish line, the crowd, arms frantically in motion, called their horse home, raised their clamorous voices even higher.

Women forgot their fancy high heels and jumped up and down. Hats flew in the air as high as the shreiks of joy! It seems horse racing fans are the same the world over as losing tickets were cast to the ground, torn into tiny pieces. Mumbles about why their winning horse didn't win and something about next time carried out too. This was pretty much the same reaction at American tracks. I felt right at home.

My first ticket did not get torn and thrown to the ground! I threw my arms out there and yelled along with the rest of them! It worked! I called my horse to come home first! And he did! My horse won! I collected Aussie money at the race track! Woo hoo!

I went back to the tent to find an empty seat at a table where the ladies called me to sit down with them. They included me in their conversation and asked questions about the States. It was easy to answer questions .

I ate a Party Pie and drank a mug of cold Foster's beer with gusto. Foster's was familiar to me from my bartending days. It became a big hit for a while in 'Jersey.

The Party Pie was new to me and fabulously delicious! It was a flaky pie crust bigger than a muffin, filled with savory, tender beef 'n gravy. My mouth watered for another one but I didn't want to appear piggy in front of the ladies. Oh, it was the best ever and the cold beer was the perfect accompaniment.

One of the gals said "You must taste a Lamington, too." Since I rarely need to be pushed into trying a new food, I reached for one sitting prettily on a plate full of them. They are finger length pieces of sponge cake dipped in chocolate and rolled in coconut. These were about two inches long and an inch wide. Hmm. Tasty.

With appetite sated, temporarily, it was time to go looking for my mate. Angelo was out at the track when I found him. He had figured out the betting, too. I had no doubt that he would. He'd had a couple winners and didn't mention the losing ones. I had a couple of those and tucked the tickets away for my travel journal.

We spent most of the afternoon but were ready to head back to our hotel when Bob came looking for us. We thanked him profusely and we exchanged addresses. To meet strangers while traveling always reconfirms my faith and love of people.

Bob gave us an unexpected grand time, a bit of synchronicity was at work on the other side of the world and down under the equator. So now I learned that synchronicity worked all over the world.

The airline delivered our carryon to the hotel while we were at the Annual Horse Race as I knew they would. My tarot card reader has never wrong, yet. We returned tired, from a fun day at the races with Australian money in our pockets. Wow! Some things are set in stone and cannot be averted.

After all the excitement of the races, we chose to go to the Great Barrier Reef the following day. It was a bit more relaxing, enjoying the peacefulness of it. Part of that trip was spent roaming around lovely, tropical Green Island at a leisurely pace. Our boat had a glass bottom showing us the beauty of the underwater at the Reef. I didn't snorkel with the others, choosing to stay above water to keep a non-swimming Angelo company. I didn't mind at all.

These exciting few days were our introduction to Australia.

Chapter 11
Australia, Part 2

"Get me out of here! Get me out of here!" Sudden loud hammering and banging noises filled the lobby! Angelo was yelling (he had mountain-strong lungs) and was banging on the elevator door creating a racket! As he descended, alone in the elevator, it got stuck between the first and second floor. He panicked!

The desk clerk nervously jumped, grabbed a bunch of keys from the wall and with deep concern on his face, ran to the elevator, inserted a key and pushed a button. The elebator came right down.

Angelo wasn't even 10 feet up from the floor or stuck for more than a minute. The hotel was only two floors high. I had to laugh at the absurdity of his panic. He didn't think it was so funny. He mumbled and groaned but didn't complain out loud.

We were settled into our hotel in Sydney in New South Wales after leaving Cairns. I went down-stairs to wait in the quiet, serene lobby where fish lazily swam in a small pool. Angelo was to follow.

I hired a car to visit some of the sites that were typically Australian. Since I used my credit card at the car agency which meant that I was the sole driver. Fine with me. Angelo looked relieved. He's not the best driver or navigator. It was my first major sojourn into driving on the left side of the road. Getting behind another car made it easier to drive until I came to turning a corner. That was the place to pay extra attention. The habit of pulling to the right was strong.

We enjoyed wandering the Sydney harbor and the cobbled lanes in the *Rocks* as the original, historical part of Sydney was called. The first European settlers were convicts, sailors, and hoodlums evicted from England instead of being hanged. Their history was well recorded and their small shabby beginning was now a charming shoppers' paradise. Many decendents of those first settlers were fully aware of their origin and proud of it.

The unique Sydney Opera House was a *must see* for me. A television crew was filming a commercial and I caught a great photo of the actors/dancers lined up at the top of the steps in sillouette. A clear, cloudless blue sky behind them framed the famous profile of the opera house.

In the early evening after showering again and freshening up, we drove out to find a good place for dinner. The sun set on this warm night and darkness fell quickly just as we stopped at an attractive restaurant. We were led to a small table that stood near the entrance of a garden. Next to it was an under-lighted, kidney shaped pool filled with large fish swimming around lazily.

"Fish ponds must be a major part of the décor down here," I murmured,

"Yea, they should put their money into elevators that work instead," he replied.

Hmm. Guess he's still a little annoyed, I thought and let the subject drop, but inside I was still chuckling.

Candle lights were scattered close to the ground along a path that circled the pool. Very relaxing, smooth music played softly. Palm trees overhung, bushes abounded with colorful yellow and red flowers. A sweet scent filled the air.

Only one other couple could be seen, seated at the other end of the pond. The entire patio area was arranged for romantic dining and privacy. The dark created a cozy atmosphere.

"I can hardy read this menu." I borrowed Angelo's reading glasses and still couldn't see even holding it close to the candle on the table.

I ordered a dish with prawns (shrimp) in it. Angelo ordered a local fish. Our chilled Chablis was served. We spoke quietly as we ate.

"Mmm. The chef knows how to use herbs. These are super!" I was oohing and aahing over the flavor of my prawns. Suddenly a bite of prawn in my mouth didn't taste like the other bites!

Uh, oh! I can't see what I'm actually eating! I kept my thought to myself. Not to make a fuss or spoil the mood, I just swallowed whatever it was in my mouth, silently praying it wouldn't poison me! After that, I was kind of feeling my way around what I couldn't see. I cut off what I thought was probably the head of the prawn. I knew it wasn't pretty, but I didn't think it would hurt me.

I didn't die. I woke up the next morning and wasn't sick either. I guessed whatever it was, it was okay. So much for romantic dinners!

We were both naturally early risers, vacation or not. This resulted in finding the wildlife park closed when we arrived at 9:30. The Park Ranger saw us at the locked gate and wandered over to appease us. A koala sat on his shouleder.

Angelo has a nice, pleasant way about him and can usually talk anybody into what he wants. He sweetly explained to the Ranger why he should let us in. The Ranger, dressed in khakis and an Aussie hat with one side folded up, told us all the reasons why he shouldn't. Then, smiling, he opened the gate, chatted with us, talking about the animals, and strolled with us for most of the time we were there. He even let Angelo hold the koala taking it from his shoulder. Signs hung around saying "Do not touch the koalas" in English and Japanese. How could I not smile?

He gave us a bag of food and left us in the center of a small field of kangaroos jumping around. There were full size 'roos and little ones and some in their mom's pouch. We fed them while the male peacocks followed us around. It was magical! The Ranger made two travelers very happy and it caused no harm to anyone to bend a rule a bit.

We wondered what the folks at home who were against our signs being printed in English and Spanish would say if they saw these signs with multiple languages. Japanese toursts were plentiful. All with cameras hanging around their necks. Travel enriches one's compassion and intelligence-in my belief. We are one world, sharing it is a good thing.

Next we drove to Manly. This was back in '87 when Manly was still a small town and we both loved small towns, especially when they carried the charm of this one. A brand new wooden walkway along the beautiful beach called to us. We strolled with no demands on our time. No schedule to keep. No one to interfere. The beach was already known for surfing. We spent an hour or two, drank lattes in a cute cafe and drove back to Sydney.

In our sauntering around, we stumbled onto a betting parlor that was rnning live horse races. Angelo perked up, made a couple bets, threw away his tickets while we drank Foster's to wash it down. It was cool listening to the Australian lingo using the same words, but sounding diferent that I heard at every reacetrack we went to.

Our next adventure followed a sign that said, *Nude beach-this way*. We followed the directions, peered from afar, chuckled at something new to our way of life and drove back to our hotel. Guess we didn't really need to pack bathing suits.

The next day we started our nine hour drive to Melbourne, Victoria which was a big part of our reason and final destination in coming to Australia. The plan was to meet Angelo's extended family and friends who emigrated from Italy in the early '50s. That was the same time period Angelo's family came to the States. He was a young teenager at the time. This was approximately 35 years later.

We set out in heavy, early morning fog. As we drove into rural countryside the fog created stunning artsy images that fueled my imagination.Iat was beautiful. It was just us on the road, no other cars could be seen or heard. As the fog lifted we saw signs that pointed to places we weren't going to, but sounded so interesting, including: Woolongong. Mittagong, Goulburn, Bundanoon, Woologorang. All were intriguing, conjuring up visions of Australian history.

I insisted we take the time to drive through Canberra, the Capital Territory of Australia. It was still morning and few cars were on the road when we arrived. The avenues were very wide. Lots of decorus vegetation grew along the way with strikingly beautiful flowers.

The avenue took us across a bridge and led us in to the National Circle that went around the State Circle that went around the Capital Circle that went around Parliament buildings. Everywhere wide, open spaces bounded on flat land. We appeared to be the only car out and about that morning.

Wide roads, like spokes in a wheel, led away from those circles to the National Library, National Gallery, and Stirling Park. We had a wide range of vision. It was clean and gorgeous in an odd way. So neat.

We didn't get out of the car. We came. We saw. We moved on. This time, Murrumbateman, Berremangra, Little Billabong, Wangaratta, and Craigieburn were place names that reminded us we were still in Australia. I loved it! I like signs and I like names.

Melbourne was a hugely spread out city. One third of the population-at that time-was Italian or Italian descent. Angelo explained to me that when World War II ended, Italy was completely deflated. There was no food and no work. Anywhere. Italians emigrated mostly to the United States, Canada, Australia, and Brazil.

Instead of building up, this enormous country has the room to build out. The residential architecture in one area we drove into made me think of New Orleans; lots of lacy wrought iron fronting the two-story houses with large front porches. For some reason this surprised me.

I had no idea what I expected. I was embarrasssed that I didn't know more about Australia before visiting. Remember this was pre-Internet days. I was a busy woman and it took time to send for brochures and visit the library for information. Plus, visiting Angelo's family and boyhood friends were the magnets drawing us to Australia.

We waited in the car after Angelo called them from the phone at the beautifully restored Victoria Train Station. station. He gave them a description of the car we drove. His cousin arrived and we followed his lead to their home. What a reunion! He had not seen his uncle or cousins for more than 35 years! Tears fell all around as he reunited with those he grew up with and believed he would never see again. They were hugging tight!

I wept just watching the love that encircled them all! Emotions burst forth without anyone trying to hold back! Excitement emanated from everyone! I could see it! Like waves bursting out!

With Italian being their first language-and many of the old timers never learned English-the King's English or American English-I gravitated to the younger set. They were 16 to 30 years of age, bi-lingual and were full of questions. This group impressed me deeply with their knowledge of the States including our politics. My heart and head had no room for politics so we moved on from there.

All of the kids were ambitious in the sense that they were hard workers, they cared, dressed strikingly, neat with style, and attention to detail. They were full of dreams and ambitions. I loved them immediately sensing the pride in their heritage, their family, and their place in the world.

Every household wanted to host a dinner for us. Wow! One of Angelo's cousins made Aarancini-balls of rice with green peas and Parmesan cheese in the center with a light coating of bread crumbs on the outside, then fried. Yum. I had never tasted them before. Again a reminder that those foods could not be found in our local food stores at home and there was no internet to introduce them to me.

Seeing this reunion made the long, (but interesting) drive from Sydney worth every kilometer. I loved being part of an Italian family at the table. It has everything anyone could want; camaraderie, homemade food at its best, deep caring, and the love just overflowed. It wrapped around me, warmed my heart, and created a bond that I will always carry. Memories.

Of course Angelo's uncle made his own wine and he gave Angelo some tips on our home wine-making process. I wasn't present when this exchange took place. Of course, maybe I was. They were speaking Italian too rapidly for me to pick up any of the words. That was okay. Angelo would share it all with me.

I mentioned that I wanted to see the Fairy Penguins. No one in the family had any idea what I was talking about. So, before we left, we found our way to Phillips Island. After parking in the lot, we looked around and saw the sign (in English and Japanese) giving instructions.

As the sun began to set a Ranger came along with flashlight in hand. By then a crowd of twelve people gathered. He spoke to us about the penguins, the natural setting we would be standing in, and importance not to disturb their routine.

He said, "You are stepping into their domain. Fair Warning! *No* cameras! We will take *any* camera and not return it if you try to take photos. Find a spot in the sand to stand perfectly still. *Do not* move even an inch, once the penguins emerge from the water. They will walk around you. Be quiet. Be still. Leave *No* trash."

We did. The penguins left their burrows at dawn, swam all day, and at dusk, came out of the water, found the burrows in the sandy rise of the beach where their little ones were nested, and fed their babies. They didn't seem to notice us. We were like immoveable trees that they just walked around.

It was most sacred. Total silence surrounded us like a cocoon. The small crowd respected this natural accomplishment. Everyone quietly left after the last penguin completed her task. I think we were all overcome by the grace of it.

The week went by in a whiz. During the last two days word had finally reached his closest boyhood friend Paolo. When he arrived at the house, they wrapped arms around each other with great emotion. Both of them wept freely, overjoyed at actually being together. They looked into the face of the other, to see the men they had grown into, in the last chapters of their lives. It was obvious that they liked what they saw.

From time to time, over the last years, Angelo told me in quiet conversations over a glass of wine or an expresso as thoughts of his youth popped into his mind. As youngsters they grew up in the terrifying fear of World War II. They lived through the memories of running to hide in fear when the bombings by the Allies began.

He mentioned one time about seeing one of his buddies pick up a shiny cigarette lighter left behind by German soldiers retreating from southern Italy. The lighter blew up, as did the boy. The picture was still in his head of body parts hanging from a tree.

He also talked of happier memories, of growing up in a small, rural, mountain village where the kids were all trained in musical instru-ments. He was proud of their town band.

At a certain age, school classes were a half day. After lunch they each had to learn a trade. He wanted desperately to become a blacksmith. His mother talked him out of it, saying it was too dirty. She sent him to the barber instead. There he learned the trade by standing on a box to reach the customers so he could cut their hair.

It paid off sooner than expected. While his mother was seasick on ship the entire trip coming to America, he was already working. It happened when he went for a haircut and learned that one of the barbers was ill. He offered, young teenager that he was, to fill in. The barber laughed and said "Try one and we'll see."

Angelo had an 'eye' and was a natural with scissors in hand. He worked everyday the rest of the trip and wound up making a pocketful of money before they reached New York City where his father would meet them.

His mother was horrified when she heard of it and wanted him to return the money. But he had earned every cent and was allowed to keep it.

As soon as they were settled in Trenton he was hired in Bordentown at Chris's Barber Shop. He was 15, not old enough to drive yet. There he remained for 45 years taking over when Chris retired.

With Paolo's family emigrating to Australia after the war and Angelo's family going to the States, they never dreamed they would ever meet again!

The next morning Qantas flew us to Tahiti.

76

Chapter 12
Tahiti
French Polynesia

We landed in Tahiti to a small airport. It was Angelo's choice to come here. I think it developed from one of his barber shop discussions when a customer sent him a post card from Tahiti showing a topless hula girl. We figured three days would be enough for this tiny island.

For me, it was interesting to explore Paul Gaugin's former home, influence, and success in Tahiti. This is where he found the happiness he searched for when he still lived in France..

Our motel was a two-story simple, but lovely dwelling with a small balcony surrounded by grassy lawns and a wooded area of swaying palm trees. When we turned on the TV, the show Bonanza came on. The Cartwright family of the '60s was speaking French!

The meals we ate at the motel were served to us in a gazebo for two, out on the lawn a short distance from the small swimming pool. It sported a grass roof. A heavily scented gardenia was placed alongside my plate. It was to wear in my hair, which I did. Very romantic.

Off a short distance a gal was swimming in the pool. She wore the straight, long, black hair of the Tahitians and she was topless. Angelo got his fantasy to tell the guys back in the barber shop! Classy as he was, he thankfully, didn't stare. He was cool. She was in the pool with us the following day, too.

Since my suit was one piece, I didn't have to make that choice. I would have acclimated if my suit was two piece. Angelo didn't seem to mind. Thankfully, again, he didn't gawk, just kind of smiled at me like he didn't know where to direct his eyes.

The following day was Saturday. We took the taxi into Papeete. Both of us were annoyed with the trash cast on the ground, in nooks and doorways, etc. It was a messy place. The trash emitted a feeling of slum to the area.

We stopped at a casual place for lunch which didn't offer much and wasn't especially clean either, so we ordered a small pizza and washed it down with two bottles of beer. $40! We drank from the bottles. (Something I never do. A beer, perfectly poured into a glass adds to its flavor.)

A Frenchman (by his accent) speaking English noticed our amazed expressions.

"You must understand. Everything is imported to us here. It is very costly."

We thanked him. It was kind of him to offer an explanation since we didn't make any verbal complaint.

There didn't seem to be a lot going on, so we asked about the bus we spotted in the square.

"It goes around the island taking people to work and picking them up. It isn't a tourist bus." He replied.

Perfect. We hopped on the bus. A half dozen Polynesians were on the bright blue, cheerfully-painted bus, trimmed in yellow and red. The seats consisted of boards placed on wood blocks, bench-style. There was no glass in the windows and there were no doors, only open doorways.

"I wonder what Allstate Insurance Company would say about this," Angelo quipped.

I had to smile.

No one else smiled. At anyone. Everyone was somber, except us. We smiled at everyone. Alas, this is the rare time Angelo could not get anyone to talk to him or respond in anyway. All eyes looked at us but no one was intimidating or obnoxious. They were just somber people wrapped up in their own lives, I guessed. They must have been wondering what in the world we were doing on this bus. People were being dropped off and picked up at different plantations where vanilla, bananas, breadfruit, pineapples, passion fruit, and guava were grown.

The dirt road was extremely bumpy. We bounced and the boards we sat on bounced. We laughed at the situation we were in. Taking a cue from us gringos, probably the only ones they ever saw on the bus, they, too began to laugh. By the time we were half way round the island, everybody was chattering and the women were giggling! I think we were accepted.

Sunday morning we waited at the airport. A honeymoon couple from Italy was the only other passengers waiting too. They were delighted that, though they spoke some English, with Angelo they could speak in their own language.

They chatted freely and expressed their amazement that for two weeks they had not eaten anything red in color! Meaning pasta, of course. They could hardly wait to get back home and have a dish of spaghetti! So much for romance.

I loved traveling but was happy to be home again. When I unpacked my suitcase, I laid it on the bed to separate the clothes into piles to be washed. Checking the inner side pockets, I found a small, medicine-size brown bottle full of a white powder. It was neatly tucked in, but not by me! It was my luggage! I panicked! OMG!

I yelled out! "Angelo! Where did this bottle in my suitcase come from?" I was frantic! I could not imagine what this was or where it came from! I had not left my luggage out of my sight just as the airports always advised!. I wondered if an airline employee had stuck it in there and didn't have a chance to take it out again. My luggage tag showed my address on the underside. OMG! Had I trans-ported heroin or cocaine!!?

Answering my agitated voice, he came slowly into the bedroom, calmly saying, "Oh, yea. I forgot. Tio gave it to me. He uses it for the wine he makes in Melbourne. It stops the wine from shedding every month. Preservative I think it's called."

I wanted to strangle him, but that's who he was and those are the things he did. Whew! I was greatly relieved. Writing this now, I wonder what a stir it would have caused at the airport today I probably would have been taken away in handcuffs and wound up in jail as the police analyzed the contents. Just how calm would Angelo have been with that happening?

Chapter 13
Fair Hill Races
Elkton, Maryland

I was never in on the planning, if you could call it planning, but I responded to Angelo's ideas with enthusiasm. Over a cup of morning coffee he said, "Get ready, we're going to Delaware today," or "Let's go to blah, blah, blah." I was up for it and *it* was always a racetrack. I think his unusual plans came from his customers. Barber shops are good places for discussions of all kinds, especially *back in the day* of an all mens' shop.

So, we were off to Fair Hills in Elkton, Maryland. I immediately thought of my mother telling me she and my father eloped to Elkton, Maryland in 1930. She made it sound very exciting. She was 15. I'm not sure my father knew she was that young. He was 21. They didn't have children for another four years, so it wasn't a shotgun wedding. When I delved into my genealogy years later, it was Norristown, Pennsylvania that they married. Duh. Mom was never a traveler.

Angelo told me that it was not a regular track but on a private farm, 'Steeplechase Races Only' Day at Fair Hills. I later learned it was an annual event, a special fund raiser, not widely advertised. These were pre GPS days. We searched for road signs from directions Angelo had scribbled on a torn piece of envelope, probably in a hurry while the next man waited for his haircut. What we found was a grassy field where volunteers directed us to park. Everyone strolled (instead of the usual charging) across the field. We followed people who seemed to know where they were going.

There were no grandstands or places to sit. Some areas were roped off as private seating and unless we had reserved seating with the hoity-toity, dressed in fancy designer clothes, we were left to wander or stand. We both worked in jobs where we stood all day so standing around did not appeal to either of us.

Angelo could not find any windows to place a bet. Racing without betting was not something anyone did in his world. Nothing here resembled the tracks familiar to us. We did enjoy the glorious, magnificent Arabians thundering along the grass, leaping over brilliantly white painted fences, clearing the ditches on the far side of the fence, racing to the finish line at breakneck speeds.

This was also the first time I saw Arabians or live steeplechase racing. These thoroughbreds were the top of the class of race horses and breathtaking to watch. It was easy to see that the horses were as thrilled at stretching their legs for a fast run in competition as were the jockeys.

I was impressed with the steeplechase run, but only mention it here to reveal that we would pop into the car and head for an unknown place if it had to do with horse racing. That was exciting to me.

This day was a highlight of the year for the wealthy set who knew each other and belonged to the same privliged, private country club. That was a different world than we moved in. As outsiders and strangers, we were left without full enjoyment. Both of us were well-dressed, but casually. No jeans. Angelo didn't even own a pair of jeans and frowned when I wore them on rare occasions.

We were a bit disappointed in Fairhill but glad we saw he Arabians run. We stayed for two races and left. It had been a one time day, not to be repeated.

Chapter 14
Delaware Park
Wilmington, Delaware

Its charm began the moment we stepped from the side parking lot to walk the path through the small wooded area over the picturesque bridge that spanned the wee creek and led to the side entrance. Pausing at the bridge for a moment was a *must-do* each time. We never entered any other way.

Going to spend a Sunday afternoon here to watch thoroughbreds run felt like stepping back in time to the Victorian age when the women wore big hats trimmed with netting and bold silk flowers, sitting on their long, piled high hair. They strolled elegantly into the Park with folded parasols to watch the horses run.

Three-generation families gathered and the kids exerted their energies before coming to the picnic area to eat what the home-cook made by hand with love in her heart. The boys would be dressed in shirts with lace at the collar and velvet shorts. The girls would be lacy with pretty ribbons flying as they daintily ran. Ah. My imagination and love of history runs away with me.

Family gatherings were still encouraged to use the picnic area. The playground area for the kids to burn off that enviable energy stood a comfortable distance away. The kids looked a bit different in their modern jeans and tee shirts, girls included. Memorial Day, July 4, and Labor Day had special events planned to encourage families to picnic at Delaware Park. They could bring their food or buy hot dogs cooked on the grill.

The various hats I wore did not have the elegance of those classic hats sometimes still worn on Kentucky Derby Day, but I could pretend. While I pretended, I picked winners! Still not a big bettor, I stuck with my $2 bets and went to the betting window to collect more often than I did at our usual tracks closer to home.

Angelo was quite surprised one day when I placed $2 bets on a specialty card offered, called a Pick 3 and won! I had picked the first winner in three races straight and one of them was a long shot! I took home something under $400!

This was quite unusual for me to make those types of bets, but when I *saw omens* on the way or had a dream of particular numbers the night before, I paid attention! The omens reminded me of something that led to something else that meant something to me. Duh. Can't explain it more than that. Didn't always work but when it did, it was fabulous!

I picked the fourth race winner too, and Angelo chided me for not buying the Pick 4 card that would have brought me an enormous win. I was happy with what I did win and refused to pine for what I didn't.

He usually did well at Delaware Park, too. I cashed one ticket for him that paid enough of a win that taxes had to be paid up front. He gave me $100 to cash it in my name. That was okay by me. My yearly income was not enough for it to make a difference at income tax time.

We ate hot dogs for lunch as was our habit. The difference being that we bought them outside at a concession stand that looked festive with brightly colored banners. Somehow food tasted better when the surroundings were cheerful and felt like celebrations.

Steeplechase races held were fabulously exciting! It was the first time I ever saw them at a public track, very different feeling from Fair Hills. The horses' particular beauty had a gracefulness all their own. It was far superior to see this live than on a TV program or in the movies. The brilliance of the jockeys' colors, the horses groomed to a sheen, on a blue sky day. A thunderous volume of voices from the crowd matched the thunderous pounding of horses' hooves as they kicked up the grass beneath their shoes. Their bodies stretched out and up to clear hurdle after hurdle heading for the finish line! They were as graceful as ballerinas.

My eyes glued to the horses and jockeys, not realizing that I was holding my breath when they leaped over a hurdle, praying that neither horse nor jockey would stumble and get hurt.

Each bit of each event contributed to making me feel like an invited guest at a special, private affair. On the Sundays when the Arabians were featured were special days. Even the outdoor barbecue concessions whose aromas wafted through the atmosphere amidst the dust flying up from the grass to meet it.

Delaware Park *was* excitingly different from other race tracks. Yes, they offered special betting combinations and ways to win, sometimes confusing to a novice like me. Their race card offered more challenges, too. Because the area was strong with an Arabian horse population, Delaware Park invited them in. I didn't know anything about Arabians, but I listened to the talk around me (eavesdropping again) and knew they were an entirely different breed and that made it special.

It didn't surprise me when I later learned that William DuPont Jr., thoroughbred enthusiast and owner of many racehorses, designed the track. Someone of his stature would include the amenities that gave the track and grounds that upperclass feel. I *was* surprised to learn that the track first opened in 1937. It had that 19th century ambiance.

DuPont was a major force who worked several years in bringing summertime horse racing and parimutuel betting to Delaware.

Both of us were disappointed when the track closed in '82 not long after we began going there on Sundays. It reopened some time later. A room set aside and filled with casino slot machines probably had something to do with the earlier closing. Neither one of us bothered with their gaming room. We peeked in once to see what it looked like before heading for our seats in the open air grandstand.

Chapter 15
Maryland Jockey Club
Annapolis, Maryland
Laurel Park

Owners, trainers and other guys who had a hand in race-horses got haircuts and many came to Angelo's Barber Shop. The race track gossip was often a buzz as he clipped away, listening and giving his opinions. He was good at telling a story, thick Italian accent and all. A long list of experiences, both good and bad was a part of his repertoire.

When one of the stories from those horse guys piqued his interest, we would be off and running. Occasionly he got a tip whispered for his ears only, not to share with his other customers. One of those occasions was about a horse running at Laurel Park. The next day being Sunday, we popped into his little pumpkin-colored Fiat Strada to chase a winner. That was how and why we drove the three hour distance to Laurel, Maryland from Bordentown instead of going closer to our usual tracks. Of course we didn't always win, but we still had fun. We were good together.

Knowing what the consequences could be, Angelo never carried a bet for a customer. If something happened that he didn't make the bet and it came in to win big, it would look like he pocketed the win or he would pay the money from his pocket to keep his good reputation. Angelo was smart, reliable, well-respected, and sensible, not at all like the movies portray horse racing fans.

Bowie Rack Track

One winter day we drove to Bowie Race Track in Bowie, Maryland with one of those tips that did win and paid a good price. The track looked a little shabby like no one cared about it anymore. We heard rumors the race course was scheduled to close. Surprisingly, since it wasn't a track we went to, even occasionly, it pulled sadness over both of us. It was like knowing a distant relative was terminally ill and his end was near.

Maybe it was the changing times. Many racetracks began to decline when gambling at casinos became legal. The buses took seniors to Atlantic City instead of the area racetracks. You could make bets on your favorite horse without going to the track. The casinos had *racing rooms* where you could bet and watch the race live. There were many factors. Slot machines (which most race fans I overhead, hated) kept some people coming to the track. The pure race fan felt the slot machines dirtied the setting. In a sense the slots helped many tracks stay viable.

Bowie did close in '85. It remained in use as a training center until 2015 long after Angelo passed away.

The Maryland Jockey Club (which owned three race tracks in Maryland) is the oldest sporting organization in the United States and devoted to horse racing. It was founded in the *colony* of Annapolis, Maryland in 1743. George Washington frequently attended the race meetings offered by the Maryland Jockey Club before he became President.

Thomas Jefferson, James Madison and his wife Dolley were avid horse racing fans, frequenting races as often as possible. They also attended the Maryland Jockey Club Dinner and Ball events hosted at the end of each meet.

President Andrew Jackson built a 10-stall stable at the White House to accomodate the thoroughbreds that he raced, entering them under his private secretary (his nephew), A. J. Donelson's name. Jackson was a member of the Maryland Jockey Club.

Presidents Martin Van Buren, John Tyler, James K. Polk, and Ulysses S. Grant were all horse racing fans and attended meets while in office. Since Grant left office, the presidents have stayed away during their terms fearing the loss of votes from anti-gambling voters.

Many presidents kept their enjoyment of the races. President Franklin D. Roosevelt didn't hide the fact that while Hitler was building Nazi Germany and Americans were struggling through the Great Depression, he listened on the radio to the live call of the race between Seabiscuit and Triple Crown winner War Admiral at Pimlico in 1938. The entire country was pulling for Seabiscuit, the horse that filled America with hope, believing if the little guy could win, they could get through the depression.

Seabiscuit did it!

Chapter 16
Florida Racetracks-
Gulfstream Park
Hallandale Beach, Florida

In the late '80s we started loosely planning a road trip to Floridafor the first week of January, every other year. We left early in the morning to avoid Washington D.C. traffic horrors and continued south stopping only to eat and stay overnight along the way. We had a destination and wanted no distractions until we arrived.

However we did stop to see Angelo's Bordentown friend Jay Thompson. They managed to play a round of golf before we moved on. Even though I was a stranger to his friends, I stayed in the house with Jay's fiancé. An older couple came to visit who appeared to be family. The woman sat in the living room next to me while the guy stayed in the kitchen to talk.

The woman asked my name.

I replied, "Arlene."

She talked for a minute or two, then paused and asked my name.

I said "Arlene." I smiled at her not knowing that she would ask me ten more times within 20 minutes what my name was. I understood. My heart went out to her very patient husband. The woman (mother, aunt?) suffered Alzheimer's disease. It was my first exposure with it. I silently sent out a prayer to those who have the disease and those who take care of them.

Two teenage girls came in who were also related to my host. I mostly listened to them because I'm rarely around teen conversation. I had no idea what to say.

One girl began talking about ear piercing and how she does her girlfriends ears with a safety pin. Perfect! I challenged her to do a second set of holes in mine. She paled. "I don't want to hurt you."

"Don't worry," I said. "I've had babies. You have no idea about hurt."

So she did! After finishing she waxed a piece of thread and slipped it through lickety-split!

Angelo and Jay returned and we prepared to get back on the road again, me with newly pierced ears!

Our next visit was to stop overnight in Hollywood to visit and have dinner with my brother Bob and his friend Joe. We were close as young kids but we've lived great distances from each other much of our adult lives. I was the glue that kept in touch with both my brothers now that we were the senior members of the family. It was good to catch up and stay connected.

Gulfstream Park was third in line before our true destination of this trip of the Florida Keys. Being in balmy southern Florida while everyone at home shivered in their parkas was heady. Having leisure time to just roam around, eat out daily and go to exquisite racetracks was sinfully delicious. The landscaping alone made an outhouse look like a place you'd want to live in.

Arriving at Gulfstream I quickly noticed there was no charging like a mad bull from the car to the track as we did in the north. Everyone strolled at a slow pace soaking in the sun, flowers, and *everything* that made it so pretty here. The perfectly arranged, brilliantly colored flowers greeted racegoers at the entrance, filled the center of the paddock area, and overflowed everywhere else. And importantly, the hot dogs were super, too.

A mile from the Atlantic Ocean that gently met the white sandy beaches, Gulfstream Park opened in 1939 to a crowd of 18,000. It closed during WWII and reopened in '44. The Gulfstream Park Handicap was first run in '46 and the Florida Derby began in '52. The quality of racing was world class. Records were set, broken and set again. In '80 Angel Cordero, Jr. set a meet record of 60 winners! My favorite jockey, Julie Krone took the record higher in '93 with 98 winners! It made me proud to be a woman!

We were there in 1996 at Gulfstream, when Julie Krone was riding Separated Love in the fourth race for 7 furlongs and won, which meant that I did, too. She repeated that pleasure in an allowance race in the sixth, up on Vashon. It was my pleasure, too. She wasn't a program pick either time, so the win paid a nice return. Ahh. That was a good January.

We drove into Key West. To make me happy, Angelo agreed to sit in the sun on the beach (fully dressed in summer shorts and shirt) while I roamed around the Ernest Hemingway Home & Museum. It didn't make sense to Angelo that anyone would pay to look inside anybody's house. I could. I didn't mind paying a fee because I knew the cost of upkeep. If I wanted evidence of those who came before me and accomplished much, I needed to joyfully pay for the privilege. For the moment we were each doing what we really loved.

It was easy to picture the big man in his house with his six-toed cats roaming in and out at their own free will which they still did. Well, descendants anyway, all with six toes on each paw.

The two-story house had lots of big windows and was basic, nothing fancy. It was also sparsely furnished. It seemed to match Hemingway perfectly. I'm not sure if inspiration came from stepping into a great writer's space or not, but it couldn't hurt. Visiting his home felt like it brought me a little closer to knowing the man whose books I'd read. His spirit was still here. It filled the house. At least that's what I felt.

Leaving Hemingway and the popular Key West sunset on the pier behind us, we drove south on the Overseas Highway, that skinny piece of land, sometimes just a bridge, over the Gulf of Mexico, Straits of Florida, and the Atlantic Ocean. The water was the same regardless which name is tagged to it. We lazed around for two days at the small, private Stone Ledge Motel on Florida Bay in the Key Largo of Bogart and Bacall fame. I wanted to practice *wetting my whistle.*

Talk about leaving spirit behind. Bogart and Bacall as a couple are long gone, but their black and white movies are still appreciated and revered by true movie lovers and artists. I loved quoting her while an image of that particular scene ran through my mind.

One day we drove to the southernmost key. We ate conch (my first time) fritters, conch salad, and conch chowder. I ate the fritters cooked from three different recipes and took some with me when we pulled back onto the highway heading north. Guess you could say that I loved them.

Calder Race Course
Miami, Florida

After the races ended at Gulfstream Park we drove into Miami to find a motel in town. We both enjoyed town life and I liked to walk a mile or two in the morning, to stretch and see what town was like. This gave Angelo leisure time to get showered, dressed, and out to buy coffee and the Daily Racing Form. When I returned to our room he would be gone I could have privacy without hurrying to dress. We would be close to Calder Race Course for the next day.

Our usual routine was for me to go in and make the motel reservation. It was 6 p.m. and we were ready to settle in for the night. We found a nice looking place in a pretty location. I went in. The neatly dressed young man behind the counter engaged me in conversation. He seemed to hem and haw a little bit, not taking my driver's license or credit card as was the normal routine.

Finally looking around sheepishly he said, "Umm m'am, I need to tell you that this motel is usually rented out by the hour only. I think you may not want to stay in Miami proper but look to the outskirts of town in more touristy areas for a place to spend the night. It will be safer for you."

I burst out laughing! I knew immediately what the clerk was telling me. This motel was for 'quickie' romances only, *to put it kindly*.

"Thank you for your good advice." I told him. "You're a gentleman for certain."

We got out of town feeling a bit like *old folk*. Since I had mentioned going to Calder the next day, he informed me that tomorrow was a dark day anyway. Miami had a renaissance since those days, though I am sure there are still some motels available by the hour, at special rates. Some things don't change.

As we headed back north and west a bit going toward Hialeah Race Track area, my thoughts dropped back to when I was a 16 year old, two weeks away from becoming a senior in high school. I took a 24-hour train ride to visit my older, bachelor brother Albert in Miami, Florida.

A block up the street from his place in a quiet residential neighborhood overrun with palm trees, coconuts, and lush tropical flowers everywhere, was a beautiful, smallish motel with an outdoor swimming pool. I could hear the voices of the gorgeous young ladies squealing in delight as they splashed around during their break time from classes on how to be the best airline stewardess they could be.

"Where there are beautiful women," Albert said, "there are jockeys."

During my week stay I heard the familiar names of Shoemaker, Arcaro, and Hartack. They happened to be jockeys my mother placed bets on with the bookies before she had to curb her expensive habit.

I walked casually by the motel a few times while my brother was at work. Peeking as I passed at the gaiety and longing to belong, longing for an exciting life. I saw jockeys having fun afternoons with girls who looked like movie stars to me.

Years later I placed bets on jockey Angel Cordero, Jr. mounts because he was originally from Santurce, Puerto Rico where that same brother later moved and lived for several years. As time passed I placed bets on him because he was a good rider. He was certainly good enough to be inducted into the Hall of Fame in 1988.

Hialeah Park
Hialeah, Florida

To us, going to Florida, was always with the horse racing season in mind. One year, at Angelo's wish, we stopped at Disney World and Epcot. No description needed. Ho-hum for me, I preferred our day roaming around St. Augustine, the oldest city in our America. We roamed San Marco Avenue and George Street in the Olde Town section, having fun taking touristy photos and soaking up history. It was founded in 1565 before my ancestors landed here on the Mayflower. The town also played an active role in the Revolutionary War. How's that for real history? My mind wandered back to books I'd read about the area, full of stories of the lives lived and died here. I would have been happy to stay there and let Angelo pick me up on his way back north.

Then we drove to the Alcazar Hotel where Angelo relaxed in the car with a glass of wine and a Racing Form so I could explore the hotel built in 1888. Being drifted back to the Gilded Age in America, absorbed the energies still there. Spirits hung around allowing me to feel the essence of place.

It was purchased and turned into the Lightner Museum, filled to overflowing with antiquities of the Victorian era, including treasured Louis Comfort Tiffany stained glass. A place with history and stories was my preference. Alas, it was time to continue south.

Hialeah has history and stories,too. Seabiscuit, the small, unlikely thoroughbred horse who became a national hero, debuted at Hialeah Park in 1935. His strength and tenacity winning race after race, beating known champions, kept hope alive in millions of Americans during the depression. It was his sheer determination to be a winner that encouraged race fans and acquired new fans who had never been to a race track. *Seabiscuit* screamed headlines in every newspaper in the country, even on the front pages.

The track was internationally known as *the most beautiful racetrack in the world* with its lush tropical flora and fauna.

Four hundred strikingly pink flamingos were brought from Cuba almost like an advance notice for the large number of Cuban refugees that came in later years.

The flamingos claimed the infield lagoon, including a backdrop of tall Royal Palm trees. The Audubon Society officially designated it a sanctuary for the American Flamingo. Hialeah was placed on the National Registry of Historic Places.

The Flamingo Stakes was born and the Widener Handicap was in place as a stepping stone to the Kentucky Derby. Society's black tie elite danced and dined at many of the Flamingo Balls on the eve of the Flamingo Stakes. In 2017 according to Miami New Times, tickets to the *Toast the Roaring Twenties* affair cost from $250 to $30,000.

In 1969 Diane Crump rode Bridle 'n Bit here, making history as the first female jockey to compete riding in a professional thoroughbred parimutuel race. She needed a police escort at Hialeah to do so. Track officials threatened sanctions against male jockeys who may attempt violence against her, taking a lesson from the year before when two female jockeys had rocks thrown at their changing trailers when they signed in to ride. (Girls had long been accepted to pitch muck in the stables, to sit the horses for warming, and for training, but not to compete.)

The jockeys screamed, "Go back to the kitchen where you belong!"

The male ego; I'm glad they learned that being beaten by a female does not make them less of a man.

In 1970 Crump rode in the Kentucky Derby as the first female to do so. She was a brave young woman who had a long career at the tracks and laid the path for others to follow.

Another of America's greatest race horses, Citation, stands proudly, full-sized in bronze in the paddock area as a reminder of his importance and the importance of Hialeah Park. It is another side of American history that is not often thought of, outside those closely involved with horse racing. Reading histories of famous racehorses told me some were born to race and be great.

It was definitely a better stop than Disney.

Pompano Park
Pompano Beach, Florida

Of course we had to stop at Pompano Park for the Standardbred races. It was like stopping in to see the relatives when we were away from home. Many of the horses here, ran at Freehold, Meadowlands, and the tracks in New Jersey. They came south for the winter. The track itself was more beautiful because it didn't have the snow, ice, and hail beating it up in the winter and it did have the usual beauty of Florida flowers and palms.

Pompano Beach was also where Stanley Dancer settled in for the winter, eventually living full time. He was sometime referred to as *perhaps the most well-known personality in the sport.* He said that he made a lot of money and was blessed with the best horses without saying how he started as a high school drop-out to devote his life to the sport of horseracing. It didn't come easy and it did come with many broken bones. He survived 32 racing spills, 4 auto accidents, a helicopter crash, and a plane crash among health problems. The man seemed to match the giants he drove. His history is as interesting and hard won as Pompano Park. The track was originally opened on Christmas Day in 1926.

There was no legal parimutuel betting in Florida at the time. The governor closed the park down, threatening *to plow it in cowpeas.* The Red Cross used the facility to assist 1,000 hurricane victims in 1928. It lay dormant until Fred Van Lennep brought the track back to life, opening in 1964 with 6,600 in attendance, stalls for 2,000 horses and living quarters for 500 caretakers. Much of the track was painted flamingo pink because his wife Frances loved flamingos. The track retained its status as the best of harness racing in Florida. We weren't there in the early years but we came to enjoy it when we did.

One year we drove the Tamiami Trail west and stayed at the Trail's End Motel in Naples before stopping to visit Angelo's brother Sante and wife Maria. They bought a vacation home in the area and enjoyed the balmy weather and relaxed winter atmosphere there.

Tampa Bay Downs
Tampa, Florida

Another outstanding memory about the Tampa Bay Downs trip was meeting up with our good friends Joyce and Del Davis from Bordentown, whose winter home was in Clearwater. Why was it that we got too busy to see our friends at home, but meet them a thousand miles away! Well, we really did get together in Bordentown, not as often as we would have liked, but always fun. Del and Angelo discussed horses while Joyce and I did our own thing.

They gave us the tour and placed the idea in our heads that maybe we might want to buy a small winter home here. Maybe even as neighbors. Hmm. Something to seriously think about when we returned home.

We women decided instead of going to the track we would spend some girl time together and go Re-Sale shopping. This was a new activity for me but Joyce knew all the best places to go.

Many times people retired to Florida only to find that they missed family, friends, and familiar places. After only a year or two, they sold all that new stuff they bought rather than ship it back north.

Tropical décor did not always fit into many northern or western style homes. Those that remained in their tropical home got a chance for fabulous bargains!

When the guys returned, they said they were treating us to dinner with racetrack winnings. That suited us just fine! We cruised through Ybor City, a neighborhood within Tampa. My heart started to beat with an instant love for this place as soon as I saw the artistic tile work, in brilliant colors, along the main street! Store front after store front was adorned with beautiful and different murals of hand painted tiles of various sizes. Original designs from divergent cultures were displayed. It was unexpected and breathtaking.

I learned later the Cubans and Spaniards first settled here were skilled cigar makers. Italians followed and learned the trade. Germans, Romanian Jews, and Chinese flooded the town next. This mix of cultures made for an interesting, thriving city. Of course, that growth took place in the late nineteenth century when immigrants were flooding in and building our country. The depression reversed the neighbor-hood status before a new surge of appreciation for the *old* that was still here.

As St. Augustine did, Ybor City kept its own personality and its soul! I believe those towns did not have their history erased by modern, soulless, boring, buildings that do nothing but house a business.

Very often in Florida if you didn't see a sign to tell you which city you were in, you had no identifying landmarks to let you know. Development overflowed one city into another. They all boasted the same stores in huge shopping centers. Chain businesses really ran the gamut. So you never quite knew where you were. No danger of that in Ybor City. They too, have the distinction of being a National Historic Landmark District.

Ybor City was shuttered for the day, so we drove north to Tarpon Springs and found another town that kept its own individual ethnic culture! They too, had beautiful ceramic tile signs and murals boasting of their town's special offerings. We walked the narrow streets. It warmed my soul with the uniqueness of place. We found a small restaurant that announced *there's a good cook in this kitche*n! That proved to be true.

The four of us enjoyed our Greek cuisine seafood dinners. The young waiter told us that many Greek immigrants came in the 1890s to dive for sponges and to work in the sponge industry. Now they had the highest percentage of Greeks of any USA city!

So I found another Florida town on the National Register of Historic Places. This was an eye opening year. I loved every minute we spent in these three places!

After breakfast the next morning we parted from Joyce and Del and spent an afternoon at Tampa Bay Downs on the way out of town. My favorite jockey, Julie Krone rode her first, serious racetrack winner here in '81 on Lord Farkle. To read the personal side of a jockey enhanced my days at the track. She became the first female rider to win a Triple Crown race when she rode Colonial Affair in the Belmont Stakes. Krone also was the first female inducted into the National Museum of Racing Hall of Fame in Saratoga Springs, New York!

Chapter 17
Saratoga Race Track
Saratoga Springs, New York

Saratoga Springs was touted in newsprint in the late 1800s as the *summer camp for the New York crowd.* Of course, meaning the rich and famous. Of course, it still held that same distinction. Of course, it didn't include us.

Saratoga Springs, New York has always been a special place. Even before the Europeans arrived on the shores of this continent, the Native peoples came to this location for the healing waters, as people continue to do today. Five years of going to the thoroughbred races here with Angelo and later ten years of coming here for the Annual International Women's Writing Guild Conferences held at Skidmore College and I never once found time to test the waters of the spas here! Go figure.

Here is a little background to give you the *feeling* of place. One month after the 1863 Battle of Gettysburg in our War Between the States, John Morrissey, known gambler and casino owner, (later congressman) organized Saratoga's first thoroughbred meet on an old dirt track off Union Avenue. It lasted four days, drew five thousand people and began a new destination and tradition.

 He invited wealthy friends, John Hunter, Leonard Jerome, and William Travers, to join him in forming the Saratoga Racing Association. Travers became President and winner of the first Travers Stakes Race (named for him) for 3-year olds. His horse Kentucky won. William Travers was toasted as *most popular man in New York* by a newspaper when he passed away in 1887.

The Travers Stakes Race is the oldest running of its nature in the USA, predating the Belmont and the Kentucky Derby. It is the highlight of the season at Saratoga.

To me, Saratoga Race Track had that historic, *old feeling* to it, similar to Monmouth and Delaware Parks. At the time we attended, the racing season was only in the month of August. That made it a summer destination.

I loved this track best of all the tracks we visited, with its' happy, celebratory atmosphere, like it *really was* a festival going on, not just the usual races. I half expected Barbra Streisand to greet us just inside the gate and burst into song as in *Hello Dolly*. The *Country Fair* feeling and appearance made it special. There were individual canopied concession booths, each flying a wee, triangular flag, on the grounds. Everything was freshly painted in happy colors.

Since Angelo introduced me to being a, *"go to the track for a hot dog lunch"* I followed his lead and became one of those fans. For those who were not, the Cutting Board concession stand went a step further with sliced fresh luncheon meat for sandwiches, etc. (Maybe the rich and famous didn't eat hot dogs?) There was a gazebo, a small jazz combo near the paddock, wine and cheese offered under a small tent, an outdoor café, and off to the side was a large, lovely kept area of picnic tables under the trees. All was tastefully done.

Saratoga was obviously the playground of the rich, the crowd that included the Vanderbilts and Whitneys. They dined in white-table clothed, now-air-conditioned restaurants inside, overlooking the track. Catering to the wealthy set was apparent but that's not what either one of us desired. (Fortunately.)

We contentedly drove the four hour trip to Saratoga Springs. Angelo was happy with any racetrack, period. I enjoyed something a little more. The racetrack was a small part of what I wanted in traveling. I enjoyed the track, but I was born to travel, to see places I read about, see how others do it, be exposed to different cultures, and ethnic backgrounds..

The first time we went, we had no idea what to expect, everything was new to us. We stayed in a cabin on the way into town. It held a double bed, a bedside table with lamp, and a small bathroom, no tub. There was just enough room to walk around the bed. That was okay. We had not planned on hanging out in the room anyway. We weren't a bathing couple either. Showering was what we did at home and it's what we did here.

The cabin was probably built in the '20s, but clean and adequate. Exorbitant August prices were in force. We were lucky to find a place within town limits that wasn't extravagant, only higher than it would be the rest of the year.

In later years we stayed just outside of town or somewhere nearby, costing much less. In the morning we drove into town and ate breakfast at a diner on Broadway before we drove into the heart of the town. We cruised around to see what the town offered to visitors and pinpoint what else we wanted to see.

The National Museum of Racing was one of the places we visited. Even Angelo was impressed. He would never have gone there on his own, but he liked the photos and descriptions, history, etc. of racing champions. I admired the beautiful animals they were and recalled my fabulous collection of ceramic and porcelain horses I bought with my babysitting money as a teenager.

We drove through Congress Park in town, enjoying the abundance of brilliant flowers blooming, definitely not tropical, but they were everywhere you could imagine!

When we walked along the main street I noticed it also sported the same theme of brightly colored flowers. The street was full of individually owned, unique shops. I only bought post cards but I enjoyed browsing. It was a grand town full of enough bustle, yet not over-crowded.

The next day at the track many of the jockeys that rode at Philadelphia Park were riding there. Saratoga was a plum for jockeys to make their fame. We saw Angel Cordero, Jr. ride and win that first day. In the future he would win there so many times that he picked up the title of *King of Saratoga*. He earned the right to be in the Hall of Fame. Jockeys also familiar from other tracks were here. Pat Day, Jorge Velasquez, Mike Smith, Eddie Maple, and Chris McCarron were riding. These were big names of the day.

When Julie Krone appeared at Saratoga, I soared! I was especially thrilled seeing her there, with the *giants* of racing. She was the first woman to ride five winners in one day at Saratoga, matching Angel Cordero, Jr. and Ron Turcotte at the time. When I was there she was still trying to bust her career wide open.

I read where she sat in the old wooden grandstands in the middle of the night at Saratoga, feeling the ghosts of fans surrounding her, some ladies boasting hats, scenting the gents' cigars and pipe smoke, and sensing the thundering of horses' hooves racing past. "It was just spectacular," she said. "You could feel it, a lot of presence in the emptiness."

As I've mentioned before, reading about the personal side of jockeys was of interest to me. It was often the grit of why one talented rider won and another didn't. It also brought the race *closer* to me. Julie Krone certainly had that grit.

Even though the horse racing sport was losing a lot of profit to the casinos, Saratoga was not losing like the other tracks. The Saratoga location and surrounds were a great destination by itself. The track daily attendance averaged at 26,000. They were second only to Santa Anita in California.

Saratoga had the knack of catering to all three groups of people; the fashion-minded-super wealthy, the vacationing working class including families, and the serious horseplayer-track man. That track man was the backbone of income for the racetracks, preferring to be at the track, but betting off the track, simulcasting at casinos, if he could not get there. Personally, I think a lot of people, mostly men at that time, who did not work on Mondays, picked up the habit as somewhere to go.

Again, I loved Saratoga and all it had to offer. There was not a year that I did not take some winnings home with me. Keep in mind that I limited myself to betting no more than $10 in one day. That did not mean several days in a row. We would not go more than two days in a row anyway.

In '87, after a couple years of visiting Saratoga, I had a different experience. On occasion, especially when I had a decision to make and wasn't quite sure of myself, my favorite psychic would do a Tarot Card reading for me. During the reading which was focused on something entirely different, she told me I would be going on a vacation where I was going to win some money. Wow! This was a first (and last) time I got a money message from a reading.

When we drove to Saratoga and settled in, this comment teased my mind. After dinner and a stroll on the main drag, we turned in for a quiet night.

The next day we were back at the track that had become so familiar to me. Like a bird pecking food at the feeder, the Tarot Card reading kept pecking in the back of my mind. I was still not about to make a big money bet, but I took my time, read the racing form, breathed deeply to let *something wash over* me. Something akin to instinct, ESP, something! That thought swirled around and swirled around in my head when three numbers popped into my mind! I played numbers 2 6 4 in a Trifecta, picking the winner, the second place horse, and the third show horse in the exact order in one race.

Down to the paddock I bounced, excitement twirling inside me. I watched the trainers give a leg up to the jockeys, I watched their lips move as they were giving last minute riding advice to the jockeys, and I watched the jockeys calmly, sometimes jokingly responding to encouragement from a fan along the parade ring.

My heart was in my throat as I walked a little slower out toward the track. I was going to watch this race track-side. I suddenly realized I couldn't see the far side of the track, so I went back into the grandstands. Of course I said nothing to Angelo, not that he would have heard me anyway. His nose and concentration were in the racing form figuring out his own bet.

It was hard to sit still. Finally the horses sauntered over and one by one entered the gate. Everyone seemed to hold their breath for that brief moment or two and then with a clang of metal releasing metal, they were off!

My first pick made a good break from the gate! He was out in front early with two horses trying to get the lead; then he was neck in neck with another and on they went, running stretched out, down the backstretch.

They came tearing around kicking up dirt, to the fourth quarter. Now my horse was pulling ahead while the others fell away. I couldn't breathe yet. Lots of space started to show between my winner, the second, and the third horse.

I held my breath! They were all in the order I wanted as they crossed the finish line!

I tensed, not certain I heard right. The announcer spit out the winning numbers and they were in perfect alignment for me! I breathed deeply while waiting for the words to be official. They did it! They did it! They came in perfectly! WOW!

I was Joe Cool walking to the window to collect my winnings and I smoothly pocketed over $365.00 for my $6.00 investment like it was something I did all the time! Whew! My dear heart did a pounding. I was exhausted!

Fate has a way of playing with me. The Tarot Card reader had also told me to be careful driving on this trip. She saw an accident, nothing serious, just to be careful. A mile from reaching home, a car rode up the right side of me on the shoulder of the road and clipped my side view mirror. There went a chunk of my winnings! Darn it! At least I had cash to pay for it.

Oh, well, it was fun winning and I still did not get hooked. Mom must have been sitting on my shoulder, whispering *don't' get hooked, don't get hooked*!

Chapter 18
Ireland, Part 1
Adventures Before
and After the Curragh

"Let's go to Ireland," Angelo said. That was all. He had no idea where to go, what to do or who to see. I think guys sitting in his barber chair came up with these ideas in between picking which horse was going to win at the track that day.

As usual I was too busy to do proper research. This was the end of August '92. No volumes of internet information available. I was managing our apartment building, two rental houses, running my gift shop which included selling on Ebay, and that was another business in itself. I was also involved in our Main Street Business group.

Neither of us knew much about Ireland; neither of us enjoyed doing touristy things when we traveled. History and seeking the soul of a place were more to my liking. Angelo was a racetrack man, a great cook, and a dancer. He liked to see, but long walks were not on his to-do list. That was about it. I also wondered how we would stay interested for ten days in a place so small in area. So I pondered a bit and zing! I'd just finished reading *Scarlett*, the sequel to Margaret Mitchell's *Gone With The Wind* fame. The book was terrific! It was unlike the later TV mini-series in '94. Hollywood completely changed the story and Hollywoodized it. Yuck. But books do feed me.

A map of Ireland allowed me to trace the steps of Scarlett, where she settled and the places she visited. I prefer small villages when traveling in foreign lands. They easily depict the character of a country much better than big cities that have the same chain stores and restaurants that we have at home. Why bother to go?

We landed at Shannon Airport in a drizzle, exchanged some money and picked up a rental car. We drove to Gort, in southern Galway first so I could get used to driving on the left side of the road again, as in Australia. This car was a manual transmission so it was a bit tricky, shifting with my left hand instead of my right.

It had been many years since I drove a stick shift. Luckily, it was a new car, easy to drive, but I couldn't figure how to put it in reverse. I do manage to get into tight places, so I needed to know how to back out. I stopped at a gas station and asked for instruction from a complete stranger. He was delighted to help a *lady yankee*. He was a gentleman with a charming Irish accent and very sweet.

We stopped at a small shop in a small neighborhood area so I could buy an Irish cable knit sweater made nearby in Galway. This was August, 90 degrees when we left Jersey but it was cold here! Rain fell in a drizzle since we arrived. A chill was coming on, though I delighted in the picturesque cobblestone streets, wet with rain. Seeing the village like this was like still shots from a movie. The proprietor also had the charmingly Irish (duh!) lilt with lots of local chatter to take with us in memory.

She suggested a pub up the street for lunch. Perfect. I ordered Bacon 'n Cabbage which was ham, shredded cabbage with boiled potato. Angelo ordered Lamb Liver. We also took her advice and stayed at Mrs. Nolan's rural Corker House. It was extremely quiet out in the country, but the relaxing atmosphere got the jet lag behind us.

The next morning Mrs. Nolan served up an enormous Irish breakfast of one egg, bacon, ham, baked beans, mushrooms, grilled tomato, and a scoop of mashed potatoes with great coffee. It was a solid beginning for a couple of adventurers. Excitement built as we headed out to see what we never saw before.

It was easy to find the M6 heading east, driving through Balinasloe. We cruised around Athlone a bit, then on to Mullingar. These were towns mentioned in *Scarlett* and I looked to see if I could find what it would have looked like 120 years ago. We both were comfortable with the feeling of *old*.

A wrong turn, which I call taking the scenic route, brought us to Tullamore. The name was familiar from my old days of tending bar and pouring a lot of the fine Irish whiskey, Tullamore Dew, on St. Patrick's Day.

Back on the right road, but still on the left side; we finally arrived in the lovely Gainstown Estate House in Navan where we stayed the night. Our suite of rooms had a small terrace outside the French doors. The Country French motif of the house had walls 1½ to 2 feet thick! The carpet, a cobalt blue was nearly as thick or so it seemed as my feet sunk when I stepped on it. The porcelain sink and toilet in the bath had blue flowers painted in; very French.

Mrs. Mary Reilly's Period Residence was as gracious as she was. The next morning she sent us off with the notable grand Irish breakfast of orange juice, cereal, one egg, slice of ham, two sausages, warm brown bread, Irish honey, white toast, and marvelous Orange Marmalade.

It was a hearty breakfast after having a fabulous supper the night before at The Flathouse-Leighton's on Railway Street. Traveling kicks up the appetite.

Looking for the Hill of Tara we stumbled on to a Welcome Center for Newgrange, a 5000 year old ancient temple built by Stone Age farmers. It's older than the pyramids of Egypt or Stonehenge of England! It is a huge mound with a narrow passageway that lines up to allow the Winter Solstice light to come through its entranceway each year, fully lighting the inner chamber within 17 minutes. Interior stone walls were covered with megalithic art. The area sites were still being discovered and uncovered when we were there.

Angelo was silent, a sure sign of interest. A group of 10 of us gathered at the entrance and Angelo stepped right into the skinny passageway. I held back as I was extremely uncomfortable, not wanting to enter, yet not wanting to refuse to enter. Goosebumps were raising on my arms.

Hesitant. I was *strongly* hesitant. The hair stood up on my neck. My head fogged. I slowly inched over the step to enter. No one looked at me as they were focused on the guide. I forced myself to move all the way into the pathway at last. I held my breath as I slowly began to follow the other 8 people who easily moved into a wider chamber. I, being last in line, barely stepped out of the passageway to enter the chamber. I hung right in front of the pathway to get out. My head was too thick to hear the guide explaining what the markings on the walls meant. He droned on about the lives of these Stone Age people who built this tomb.

I already knew what information he was about to reveal. Was that why I was fearful? I already knew about these markings, but how? Not in this lifetime. Before he indicated that he was finished or took a step forward, I scrambled out of there first and fast. Outside, I breathed deeply to be free and in the open air again. Still, no one seemed to notice, including Angelo.

Leaving Newgrange we found the Hill of Tara nearby. We both walked over the hill. I let the sensation wash over me, wanting to feel what Alexandra Ripley wrote about her hero, Scarlett's excitement at seeing her father's beloved Tara. We walked around on our own, after going through an iron gate that let us in, but would not let the grazing sheep out.

I could feel Ripley's excitement as I walked around that green hill, allowing my senses to talk to me. Vibrations emanated from the ground. But if I had not known it was the Hill of Tara, it would have appeared to be another green patch of Ireland. I have since wondered if more had been done to mark the area for the greatness that it contained.

A small busload of people came including a woman from Princeton, New Jersey-18 miles from our hometown of Bordentown. She spoke clearly that she was there because of *Scarlett,* too.

Amazed to run into someone from home, we spoke briefly about Ripley's book before I spotted a small area of tombstones next to St. Patrick's country church. I walked directly to it expecting some really old ones. Tombstones tell the history of people who leave their mark on a place. The oldest was a black marble with a metallic gold lettering dated in the 1880s! Wow! That's not old! There were a few from the 1980s, too. I had no idea what they did with the ones who died before.

The River Boyne flowed around and through this whole area, moving eastward to Drogheda. To see this river that has flowed in and out of my life from reading about it over many years and its tremendous importance to Irish history covered me with awe. Ireland already overflowed me with emotion and we had only been here a few days!

We drove to Trim, another of *Scarlett's* towns. This area had lots of castles, many tumbling down in various degrees. Some were being restored. A few were open to the public. It was strange, yet thrilling to drive down the road, glance over and see a castle. Sometimes it would be a huge pile of rocks, a reminder of a predominant style of life that ended long ago. Yet it was all so familiar and comfortable.

As I looked through the open car window to a quiet countryside it was spotted with the excitement of leftover Renaissance jousting. Those competitions were unseen today except for the special Country Faires the villages held. My childhood was spent in many castles, all of them in books. I feasted on them. They were the romance of the Middle Ages.

The grand breakfast kept us from stopping for lunch but we did find a spot to relax over a pastry and coffee. That bit of rest let the lingering of this magical land of castles and knights in shining armor set within me. This area impressed me deeply and I was hesitant to leave. Being in County Westmeath and County Meath fed my soul.

The R154 to M3 brought us into Dublin, a beautiful, clean spread-out city, vibrant with life. The light traffic made it an easy time to just cruise around, get the *feel* of place. This city was much easier to drive in, than most foreign cities I've dared to enter, tucked into a rental car. The cleanliness impressed me. The few B & Bs that I enquired were full, so we decided to go just south of Dublin to Bray. The seaside town was an easy 25 minute drive. It was simple, plain, clean, and very inexpensive.

We dined at the Grove Inn, seated in the lovely Blueberry Room full of warmth and welcome. Angelo ordered grilled salmon. My Cod Florentine had a whipped cream cheese-spinach base, thick slice of cod and a creamy cheese sauce over all. Fabulous! We needed a bit of stretching after eating so we walked along the edge of the feisty Irish Sea. Angelo wore his jacket and I kept my super warm Irish knit sweater wrapped around me. What a great buy that was! Yet astonishingly, we saw kids swimming in the Irish Sea!

We returned to the B & B and Angelo began talking (he always found someone to talk) to another visitor. The man and his family came from Hamburg, Germany on his five week annual vacation. That was a perfect example of why I love to travel. Here was an American, a born and raised Italian, having an hour long chat with a German in an Irish B & B. Does life get any better? There is plenty of room for all of us on this planet we share. I also thought *how nice to see a family explore together and not on a trip every year to Disney.*

I was grateful for this experience of friendliness between foreigners, meaning all of us gathered here. Travel outside one's own country is so enlightening.

Chapter 19
Ireland, Part 2
Our Adventures Before
and After the Curragh

An announcement came midway before we finished our full-plated Irish breakfast in Bray. The taxicabs of Dublin had blockaded all streets into the city. (This continued all during the '90s.) The taxi drivers protested tough regulations keeping them from earning a better wage.

On this day, it was to our benefit. When we entered Dublin center, the streets were nearly empty. Our first stop was St. Patrick's Cathedral located right in the middle of a friendly, retail area.

My tenant, Sandra Lee, asked me to please bring some holy water from St. Patrick's. Being Catholic it held special meaning to her.

I looked all around the interior of St. Patrick's for a font with holy water. Though I am not Catholic, my high school girlfriends were, so I knew exactly where they should be. Hah. With a red face, I asked, and learned, St. Patrick's Cathedral was not Catholic, it was Protestant! That was a bit embarrassing. Who knew? Apparently Sandra Lee didn't know either.

Not to go home empty bottled, I went around the block to fill it with the holy water of St. Nicolas Cathedral of Myra. At least she would receive holy water from Ireland. (This time *I* put the wee bottle in my suitcase. The drug-sniffing dogs at the airport went right by me without a glance.)

Vendors were lined up on the sidewalks displaying their wares. We strolled the street empty of cars for awile. Fresh fruit, vegetables and anything else anyone may want was available, at good prices. Angelo loved open-air markets. He was thrilled to find greengages, a member of the plum family. He bought one for each of us and savored the taste of this fruit I had never heard of! It was delicious.

A week in Dublin would have been nice, but, alas! We were on our way in early afternoon, heading for the gateway to County Wicklow, Enniskerry. We drove into the small, lovely village, stopped at the monuments in the center of town to take photos, but did not linger.

Next along the way was Glendalough, the remains of an ancient monastic site founded by St. Kevin in the 6th century. I whipped the car right into the carpark. It was time for Angelo to enjoy a relaxing break in the car.

I roamed, deep in thought allowing time and stone to seep into my body; a spiritual trip through the ages of this tumble-down leftover of a small city. The oldness settled into my bones. Tears welled up and goosebumps surfaced my skin. Relics were left to explore, to touch, to feel what once was. A stone bridge was set off a way and started my heart to flutter. Stone bridges affect me that way! They are ignored wonders of perfection from an ancient time that our modern-day does not even notice! A small bird sat on the bridge and watched me quietly, not singing.

The stone and rock were pitted with time. Age was showing, making it more beautiful than any modernized town. I walked through the medieval stone gateway. It was remarkably intact, each stone cut to fit. No mortar was used to cement the stones in place. A stone wall once surrounded this once, old, city.

Parts of the walls remained, at various heights, as did parts of seven churches that once stood tall. I read, that one of the churches was built in the 11th century, one in the 12th. The remains and tumble downs were preserved and gave an inkling of how life once existed.

Tenderly, I stepped into the reality of another time, entered, paced, saw, touched, and heard a stillness of time. It brought an old excitement to life. I shivered on this warm afternoon.

St. Kevin's Kitchen, the affectionate name for St. Kevin's church was still standing. The Round Tower was surrounded by tombstones that *were* old. The tombstones had the appearance of concrete and stone mini soldiers standing upright, some leaning, gathered in one place to watch over their land. I let what my eyes saw soak into my soul. It's familiar to me. Why? What have I forgotten when I was born into this lifetime? I continued to walk thoughtfully, in reverence for this sacred, peaceful place in the world. I would like to return here again one day. Completely sated I returned to the car.

Angelo never asked what I saw or thought. Maybe because Italy is so old with its own stone left-behinds. Maybe he just had no interest and let me be to respect my own interests. I remained quiet as I drove down the mountain from Glendalough heading south toward Arklow, we passed through high, green hedges grown close to both sides of the road. Trees overhanging the roadway created a long, shady, natural tunnel. Cool!

Arklow gave us another special, personal memory by our witnessing a tradition that I've not seen in the States. After we settled in at the charming, beautiful Fairy Lawn B & B of Rita Kelly, with me oozing pleasure over the textured wall-paper and big, comfortable bed, we took our appetites to Main St.

Strolling along the main street in town, window shopping along the way, a shopkeeper drew down the shade of her doorway and locked it as we stood in front of it. Then another did the same as we approached. A funeral procession proceeded up over the hill toward us. The hearse drove slowly, pacing itself for the large group of people walking behind it.

I heard the click of the door lock behind us as we respectfully stood curbside in the late afternoon. Traffic was backed up as far as we could see. It was quiet, no horns blared in complaint; no one spoke. They silently passed by.

Within 5 minutes, shop doors were unlocked, shades raised, and the street filled with smiling people again, buzzed with conversation. Respect. A wonderful moment to experience.

We continued down the street to the welcoming, friendly Marine Restaurant for supper. Angelo savored a steak. My Battered Cod & Chips still had the taste of the sea. What better place to have seafood so close to the Irish Sea?

The stroll back to our B & B was a pleasant way to settle our dinner. The number of people on the street had thinned but there were still a few to smile and say hello to us, two strangers.

The next morning the cozy breakfast room had a low buzz on the wireless (radio) giving local information. A murmur of conversation flowed. This moment felt surreal, like we were all actors in the opening scene of a movie. I was bursting with gratefulness to be part of this morning.

A couple at a nearby table spoke to us. "Good morning. How are you enjoying Ireland?" I guessed we stood out easily as not being Irish.

Angelo was happy to answer and added, "Can you tell us if any horse racing is nearby?"

The Irish gentleman was delighted to give directions to County Kildare, Newbridge with a grand smile on his face that matched that of his lady's.

Fresh, hot coffee and tea were offered at this beautiful table laid with an Irish linen cloth. Fresh flowers filled a small vase. The usual, full Irish breakfast was set before us. In the middle of our table sat an elegant stem glass filled with marmalade. *A nice touch*, I thought. The room was lined with tall bookcases filled with reading material. A large window beamed bright sunshine. Congenial travelers gave us cheery smiles and hand waves. It was a great way to begin any day.

Confident now with a horse race destination and a hardy breakfast under our belts, we packed up quickly. We drove back north again, but westward away from the Irish Sea coastline.

Gorgeous mountains surrounded us. Up mountains and down mountains, through lovely wee villages we went. No time to linger now. Angelo had horse racing on his mind and would not calm down until we got close enough to smell them. He anticipated hearing the encouraging "c'mon!" of the race fans calling out to their favorite horses.

A few hours later, we pulled into Newbridge onto busy Main Street and a curbside parking spot, practically at the front door to the family-owned Curragh Inn. The sign stated it clearly. Stretching first as we left the car, we stepped out of cold sun light into darkness inside a bustling restaurant. Still full from breakfast, we went straight to the bar and luckily found two seats.

A handsome, congenial young bartender greeted us, "Welcome! I'm Andrew, one of the sons in the family. And I can tell you're Americans!"

How could he tell? We hadn't even said hello yet. He took the time to chat with us even though the place was crowded and he was busy pouring drinks and answering questions in between.

"If all the sons of Ireland came home from other countries, we'd have no room for 'em." He said. His lovely Irish lilt overflowed while making the best Irish Coffees that warmed us to our toes!

Angelo engaged him in conversation about horse racing, where we hailed from, etc. Lovely man that Andrew was, he blessed us with two free grandstand entrance tickets for The Curragh Racecourse!

Since The Curragh Raceway didn't open until the next day, we decided to search for Leopardstown Races. The horses were running that afternoon. We headed back toward Dublin's outer rim, anxiously stopped five or six times to ask for directions as we continued to get closer.

Angelo excitedly panicked that we might not find the place in time! He brought to mind the times when I wanted to get to a theatre early for a live performance. It was the same way with him. He liked to be there before the start of any event.

I spotted a car with a *Pick Six* racetrack sticker on it and blindly followed it for approximately 8 miles. He led us right to the front gate of Leopardstown Racecourse! Bingo! I guess all those whodunnit books I read taught me how to look for clues. Several double decker buses were parked in the lot. Whew! The first race had yet to start! We made it!

It had been raining with heavy gusts of wind, but the rain stopped soon after we arrived. The wind dried the track a bit. Track conditions affected the race because some horses liked to run on the muddy track and others did not.

The betting took place with individual bookmakers outside, all in a line along the track, each with their odds posted on a pole-type set-up. It reminded me of the racetrack bookmakers on our trip to Cairns, Australia.

The jockeys' colorful silks added to the exciting festival atmosphere. They looked grand atop the huge horses stepping along, almost like the horses were performing a prancing dance. They had a proud air about them, like they knew how beautiful they were.

The racing form was given at the entrance, but I also bought an In-Form for one Irish pound to read what someone who knew these horses and jockeys, thought about who was going to win. He stated that Political Fact had not raced since last October, liked soft going (wet track) and could win this race. Sounded good to me. I took his advice; placed 2L (Irish pounds) bet on Political Fact. He came in first! I won!

His next pick was Shandon Lake. He was the best of the runners here but possibly overrated. *What the heck,* I thought. I put a 1L bet on him. I won again! Darn. I should have bet more! I liked this racetrack. The next race I placed 2L on Poolesta who the In-Form said was clearly the best of this trip. For the third time, I won! Wow!

That was the end of my winning streak. I lost 1L on the next race and decided to go home a winner even if a small one. Plus we planned to go to the track the next day, too.

The horse racing in Ireland and Australia was probably a bit familiar because I read many of the Dick Francis novels over the years. As a young man, he was a steeplechase jockey (called jump-jockeys here) even riding on Queen Elizabeth's mounts for a few years. He, with his wife Mary, wrote detective novels with horse racing as back story from 1962 until 2000 when she passed away. His son Felix left his teaching career to co-author the detective stories until 2010 when his father passed away. He has carried on his parent's legacy.

We stayed for all seven races. I went down to watch the horses come from the stables to the track, watching other people's expressions as they won or lost, loving every bit of it, an easily contented woman.

Just being at the racetrack contented Angelo. The smile on his face told me he won.

"A little bit" he said. He was never one to tell me how much he won or lost. That was okay.

Chapter 20
Ireland, Part 3
Our Adventures Before
And After the Curragh

All the B & Bs were filled on the way back to Newbridge. It was late in the day for stopping. I wasn't worried, we had both been lucky at the track so I knew we would continue having a lucky day.

Finally we found a room available at the Kerryhill Guest House. The lady was gracious, kindly, and made a fire for us before we returned from having a pizza and Pepsi supper. No fussing. We were both tired. It had been a long, exciting, memorable day.

The next day was Sunday. This wasn't a B & B, so we stayed in bed until 10 and checked out before noon. No places of any kind were open so we skipped breakfast. We could lunch at the Curragh, *Home of the Classics* and the famous *Irish Sweep Stakes Derby*. It was a famous and exciting place to see.

We arrived at 1:30 in rain that turned into heavy downpours. Strong winds continued to blow even after we got inside the grandstand. (The Curragh has since been enlarged, modernized, and improved.)

Ye Gads! A mild case of diarrhea hit me, not disastrous but uncomfortable; distracting. Between running to the ladies room and trying to make a bet, I was miserable. My intuition did not work that day. How could it, with my nervous mind some place else? I lost the first two races and called it a day. It would be better to spend time reading the racecard also given to us without cost. That meant I already considered myself a winner.

Seven races were offered with five to thirteen horses running in each race. Angelo had a super day, winning more than yesterday! He smiled bigtime, a sure sign.

As we pulled away from The Curragh going south, the sky cleared. My diarrhea cleared too, thankfully. Maybe my body was telling me to not lose the Irish money I won the day before.

It took about an hour before our stomachs began to growl. Loud. We had no immediate destination or time schedule. I was driving casually enough into County Tipperary enjoying the beautiful Irish countryside. As I approached and drove around a curve - WHOMP!

It seemed like a gigantic stone rocket suddenly popped up in front of us! The gray of ancient rock emerged out of the emerald green grass of the day's rain and made a dramatic monumental appearance!

The sign noted the Rock of Cashel. A sudden, strong sense came over me. I *needed* to go inside this castle! Reluctantly, with both of us exhausted, even though I was antsy, I agreed to wait until morning.

The nearby O'Grady Rockview B & B drew us in as it exuded a lovely, welcome feel from it. We could gaze at the Rock of Cashel from the bedroom window. Mrs. O'Grady commented on how romantic it was.

It was an easy walk into town from our lodgings, but all the Pubs had to offer in the way of food were ham and cheese sandwiches. We finally caught on that the Pubs offered a more substantial selection of foods in early afternoon. Not tempted, we continued our walk and luckily found Alice's Bistro.

Angelo and I were both lovers of good food. We entertained at the dinner table at home with both of us cooking and we loved going out to taste how someone else cooked. For Angelo, the Irish table was a whole new avenue of cooking, so different from his southern Italian palate. For me, my avid reading and thirst for how other cultures cooked the same basic foods I cooked, was fulfilling a deep desire.

Angelo was happy to see grilled lamb on the menu. I loved lamb but continued to order battered fish and chips. I wanted to get my fill of it while we were here. (Years later, I walked down the street eating battered fish and chips wrapped in newspaper the old fashioned English way. A custom fast disappearing.)

Alice topped our dinner off with the best handmade Lemon Meringue Pie and cheesecake. Since we were the only customers that night, she supplied us with good conversation. This was the perfect way to finish the day. Talking with people who lived here was the best way to get to know a place. You cannot get it any other way other than being here. Period.

Excitement rattled my bones as I woke the next morning. My dreams were full of the Rock of Cashel. The monument of Celtic history was my first waking thought.

I had not bugged Angelo about touring most of the places we passed, knowing he had no interest. He was fine with my insistence on seeing the interior of this castle. He was content to relax in the car in peace and quiet. Steps were breath-taking for him and there were many steps just to get up to the entrance from the empty carpark.

The gentleman at the door allowed me to roam on my own since no one else was about. Once inside the castle I let the essence of place soak into my heart. Again I could feel the time past as a sensation. It ran over and through my body. I must have been here before. I wasn't overwhelmed with happiness or sadness, just feeling a life being lived.

Only limited areas were available to enter. Simplicity ruled. Much bareness of stone and stucco dominated, with the sparse, massive, clunky wooden furniture pieces one expects in an ancient castle of power. I learned later the power that challenged Tara for control of Ireland was in this place.

Aged, worn tapestries adorned the walls. I knew in medieval times they were woven by hand on looms. Often the ladies of the court stitched a design or *cartoon* for years before it was finished. When hung, the tapestry acted as insulation retaining some warmth in the room and the cold out. Doorways were hidden from plain view. Tapestries covered beds for warmth while sleeping on those cold, wet winter nights.

Today the deep thickness of the walls kept the interior quite chilly and the tapestries kept the heat out. The pamphlet I read the night before prepared me with some history. I wandered slowly, wondering about the Kings of Munster who lived here and about the one king who eventually gave the castle to the church. Why did he need to curry favor from the church? I wished I knew more Celtic history and art. St. Patrick visited here at least once. That fact alone added importance to the Rock of Cashel.

Drifting around the Romanesque chapel I stepped outside where the cluster of medieval buildings snuggled in close. Old, pitted tombstones filled the lot. Surprisingly, the oldest date was 1777. Whatever did people do with their dead long ago?

That outside area called me to meander around the tombstones with love swelling in my heart; a caring about those bodies buried on this grand hill. Lingering here as the sun was rising in the sky lay a sense of time on my shoulders.

It's typical ancient Ireland, so a stone wall surrounded the property in varying heights. Stone walls piqued my sentiment. They settled my attention on the word *permanence.*

My thoughts came back to the present, time to move on, to leave the past behind, to rescue Angelo from solitude.

The Tipperary Races were next on our list, stopping a half hour east in Clonmel first. We walked this pretty little town still bustling from yesterday's music festival. We missed it, but enjoyed the bits of music still being played on the street. It was easy to tell the few people wanderiang were leftover stragglers from yesterday. They carried a 'not quite awake to reality' look about them, not wanting to part from a happy time too soon.

An interesting two-wheeled cart, painted a glossy black, trimmed in shiny gold lettering announced baked potatoes for sale. It was the cutest thing!

Within 10 minutes of leaving Clonmel, on the way to Mitchelstown, I thrilled to spot a caravan of Travelers, who some call Gypsies, coming around a wide bend from a side road toward us! Their waggons (i.e. their spelling) were rounded, sort of tube-like, brightly painted and decorated, probably by one of their own. They must have been in Clonmel for the music festival!

I read that all the waggons of old (like this one) were no longer in use. The Travelers in the States were all using motorized campers now. European Travelers, too. So this was an uncommon sight! It was so exciting, like stepping back through time, into one of the novels I read long ago, but whose essence still stayed with me.

A man, woman, and child sat up front. He was holding the reins of the horses. The details painted on the waggon were easy to see because of the brilliance of colors. I wanted to stop the traffic and introduce myself, but had not lost all my mental marbles yet! I wanted to tell them how much I admired that they stood to their ways and had not assimilated to a way of life they don't accept. Individuals are so rare these days. Annoyed traffic pulled around them.

Both the man and the woman wore a white peasant, full sleeve shirt. Her red skirt trimmed prettily in a floral design, flowed across the front of the seat. Her hair was contained in a scarf tied behind her neck. Her large golden hoop earrings flashed in the sunlight. I strained to hear the bangles on her arms, but traffic noise interfered.

The small child was between them. *Passionate and thinking individuals are alive and well,* I thought to myself. Angelo did not understand any of this. He saw things differently than me. He would not understand how seeing these Travelers and waggons excited me even more than race horses did to him. His response would be abrupt and I'd be offended. So I didn't share my thoughts.

Next we backtracked northwest less than an hour away heading for the next racetrack, only to find that the races were in North Ireland today and Galway the day after. Oh, my!

Again, we drove in the opposite direction, heading south for about 45 minutes to Mitchelstown. We stopped for lunch at O'Callaghan's Delicatessen who offered a great Shepard's Pie filled with lots of ground lamb, vegetables chopped tiny in rich gravy, and a thick topping of mashed potatoes with a hint of cheddar in it. Yum! The aroma when the young lass placed it on the table was enough to make me drool.

Even the foods offered delighted me because they were foods I read about but never saw offered in the States.

If it were, it would not have the authentic taste of its own country. The food was a part of our experiencing travel abroad. If you don't meet the people, eat their foods, and sleep in their houses, you have not truly touched the soul of the country. O' Callaghan's is still there today, expanded to include a bakery and café! Amazing!

Feeling filled with good Irish food again, we drove south through Fermoy and arrived in Cork at 4 p.m. This is a city of 135,000 people. Much larger than expected. A wee bit of time driving around the southern portion gave me the feel of the city as I enjoyed doing; didn't stop, but continued driving south to Kinsale.

Located on the southeastern coast in County Cork, Kinsale was totally different from any Irish town we'd been so far. Perhaps because it was a sea town with an international feel to it, invitingly picturesque, with oodles of restaurants and pubs.

Anxious to walk the town, we secured our lodging at McCarthy's Hilltop B & B first. It sat in a great hillside location that overlooked the town and the harbour. (i.e. Irish spelling) Down to the White House we strolled where we ordered a couple of half pints of lager and Guinness mixed. A fellow was playing the accordion, then the sax rather badly. No one cared. All were having such fun. We sat in the middle of this camaraderie laughing and adding to the comments long after we ate supper.

Charmed by the participation of happy people abounded! Kinsale crept right into my heart. We couldn't let the night end just yet. So we visited the swans gracefully floating on the water. Enchanting.

Sparkling stars in the night escorted us back to the B & B where we met a couple from Boston, Texas. An enjoyable hour in conversation with them followed before retiring to bed where sleep came quickly and soundly. It was a beautiful, perfect day that left me feeling extremely grateful and happy with my life.

Dawn brought brilliant sunshine that continued to shower happiness as it flooded the B & B dining room. A few chatty words with our new friends of last night carried on the intimacy of place. Meeting a fellow countryman, even as far from us as Texas, brought a warm feeling of pride of being American. Especially nice, polite and respectful folks such as they were. Loved it.

A hearty breakfast was served in the graceful dining room gleaming with white cloth-covered tables, shining flatware, pretty dishes light in color with dainty flowers painted on them, and sparkling glasses.

Starting our day with grace became custom. Travel is great for the mind, body, and spirit. Still hesitant in leaving Kinsale, we took another walk through town. We both loved this place!

Reluctantly we packed the car, pulled onto the road and were on our way to Clonakilty, still in County Cork but referred to as West Cork.

Clonakilty also overlooks the Irish Sea and turned out to be another charming town to walk in, so we did. We window shopped at small, individual, freshly painted stores designed with 19th century charm, that were probably built then. Seeing the variation of traditional Irish cable knit sweaters, accessories, and all the beautiful items Ireland honestly boasted about was lovely. I wanted to buy lots of items but needed to control my urges.

Angelo enjoyed seeing how the butcher shops laid white porcelain trays of fresh cut meat in the windows. The bold colors of fresh vegetables and fruits displayed at the produce shop showed the same care and artistic flair for design worked into their daily chores. Everything appeared to be locally grown.

A tea room sign called to us. Um, we stopped for a pastry and wound up sharing some variation of delicious lasagna for lunch. The pastry and a scone was slipped into a bag for later.

I drank my coffee with cream and sugar, which I never did at home and enjoyed it to the max! I knew if we stayed the day and night here, we would have fun, but time was on the downside now and more places beckoned us. Heading south, a sign announced Skibbereen! Irish town names were cool so I couldn't bear not to stop. We didn't stay long in the pub, but had fun talking with the locals as they explained "the half pints we ordered cost the same as full pints. They were considered ladies and old men's drinks because it takes them so long to drink them."

The gents were so good-natured that we laughed instead of telling them that we were really wine drinkers. Besides, Angelo said, "It isn't real money if it isn't Yankee dollars. Ah. In Ireland we did as the Irish did.

Chapter 21
Ireland, Part 4
Our Adventures Before
And After the Curragh

We drove west into the rain where we pulled up in Kenmare, the Jewel of the Ring of Kerry. This was a destination Angelo's customers assured us to visit. We came to find out why.

First, the rain ceased to fall, so we walked the town a bit letting Angelo again drool over the small butcher shop that displayed its freshly cut meats in the window and the grocer next door its fresh fruits and vegetables. That was something we no longer saw in the States. I think it reminded him of growing up in Soveria Mannelli, a small mountain town in Calabria, Italy. We carry so many images of our childhood lives that simply disappear until we see something to remind us.

Again a pub magnetically called us for a couple of half pints. While Angelo relaxed in conversation with a local fellow, I trotted across the wet street into Quillen's Woolen Market where I drooled over the most gorgeous knitted items, but I could not justify spending the money. I loved seeing the real thing, though. It was like going to an art gallery to enjoy original paintings compared to prints seen hanging in furniture stores.

I collected Angelo and we got back on the road. Quite unexpectedly, we were now driving in the mountains! I didn't see them coming. They just sort of appeared out of nowhere and we were on top looking way down at the sea below. I had not realized we had risen so high in altitude. Even the rain did not mar the spectacular panorama! Weather had not deterred tour buses, either. There were plenty of them, not a pleasant sight after this past week of little traffic, even in Dublin, and lovely small towns. Yet they did not detract from the breathtaking beauty of the area.

I had no idea we were already *on* the Ring of Kerry. We entered it at Kenmare. We were going from sign to sign using general directions.

At 5 p.m. we entered Killarney and found Mary Murphy's Greenmount B & B on Rock Road for a much needed rest. Driving was tiring or maybe it was the altitude.

We relaxed for awile then walked into town, delighted to be out of the car and up on our feet. The blowing wind and rain had been coming off and on again. If we were anywhere else we would have considered it a miserable day. But, it was Ireland and everyone ignored the rain and just lived with it, so we did, too.

Angelo ordered Pasta Bolognese at the restaurant we found and I continued with seafood, ordering a fresh Monk-fish lightly breaded and pan-fried. Both dinners were perfect.

My old habit of eavesdropping brought foreign languages to my ears. Angelo was tuned in, too. I think he picked up my habit. And enjoyed it.

We could hear several different languages being spoken, German being the predominant one. Outside, the street was full of visitors. We joined the crowds and walked around the town while the night was between rainfalls.

The following morning, bright and early, after our breakfast, and filling the gas tank, we set off to continue driving the Ring of Kerry. Since we had driven part of it yesterday and not wanting to backtrack, we took the counter-clockwise route. Neither one of us had *any* knowledge of this area at all. We had no idea what to expect except we thought it would take an hour or so. Hah! We just kept looking out the windows murmuring at the beauty of it. Looking down, the views were stunning, the sky, the green of deeply dropping grass hillsides, and the water, glistening at the bottom. The land unrolled a huge drop down and ended into the sea.

As we drove, I realized this was becoming a much longer drive than we anticipated. Angelo was an energetic man. He became truly antsy after an hour and a half. His patience level was nil. He started complaining about how many beautiful views did we need to see? I was getting annoyed. It's not like I could just make a turn at the corner. There were no corners. The road wasn't wide enough to turn around and we already drove over 2 hours. How long can this road be?

Then I saw a road sign that said it cut through the Ring. I turned on to it thinking it was a short cut. We both agreed it had to be shorter than all the way around. Of course we had no idea what part of the Ring we were in!

He continued to complain. I became more nervous. The stunning views soon became a horror! The winds blew strong enough to rock the car! I was afraid it would blow the car and tip it over! We were on a narrow ledge on top of world!

The road narrowed, falling away on both sides, with no shoulder! Apparently no one here had been introduced to guard rails. If they don't help, at least they gave the feeling of protection.

I used my peripheral vision because I dare not take my eyes off the road! As we progressed, I now slowed down to 5 miles an hour, Angelo kept yelling at me to stop going so fast! My knuckles were white, gripped to the steering wheel! This was the most terrifying drive I ever took!

The road began to narrow even more to what looked like 6 feet wide! Soon it turned into dirt and stones! I didn't know what to do! I couldn't turn around and I had no idea what was ahead. Did the road disintegrate? Would our little car be too wide for an animal track? What would I do if another vehicle came up the road? Why wasn't there a sign preventing us from taking this road? Why didn't we talk to someone about this last night? What were we thinking? How could we be to out of touch?

A slight twist would cast us over the side to a certain, painful death! We crept on, me trying to block out Angelo's shouting. Thankfully the strong winds stopped and the sun came out.

After creeping along, slower than I ever drove in my life, what seemed like ten hours, the road became a macadam 2-lane again, widened to whatever was normal. Whew! I breathed deeply trying to calm myself. I was shaking. A sweat rolled down from my forehead.

A car came toward us on a lengthy straightaway. I silently thanked whatever angel was with us because that was the only way I got through that mountain road! I thanked the angels that kept the cows and sheep away, the ones who often refused to get off the road. Fortunately they stayed down in the meadows at the bottom of the mountains not up where we were.

Soon two more cars passed just as we reached a macadam outcrop where a few buses were parked. We were back to what appeared to be the normal road again.

Buses, big, wide tour buses! *Thank God* none of them approached us on the road! I wanted to kiss the ground! Angelo wanted to get back to some kind of civilization. We had been on the Ring of Kerry for at least 6 hours! We had not stopped along the way to look at anything. Whew! I hoped I would never have another day like this one. It was a high price to pay to see beauty!

Two grateful people, Angelo and I, arrived in Killorglin. (I recognized this name years later when I watched the Ballykissangel series on TV.) This could not have been a more welcome town to settle for a couple pints of lager and the best Irish soup ever at the Bianconi Pub. I was delighted to learn later that it eventually became an Inn, still serving fine food from the reviews I read online. Seeing it brought back warm memories. We were hungry travelers thrilled to be back in civilization, our feet on firm ground, and doing normal things, like eating fine food again.

We strolled through this lovely town, happy to be out of the car and on level, dry land before we got back on the road. Me? I was thankful that we were not at the bottom of one of those mountains, all broken, bleeding, and dying.

It was many years later that I looked at the map of the Ring of Kerry. If we had not taken the short cut, we would have had places to stop, to park, towns to walk around. Just thinking about the Ring of Kerry, I still feel the terror I felt that day.

Limerick City in County Limerick was our new destination. We arrived at 4 p.m. to lots of noise and traffic so we moved on to Ennis, County Clare where we started our journey.

The charming Teach na Feile B & B, proprietor Mary Galvin, was our choice to stay the night. I couldn't pronounce the name properly, but how Irish could we get? Recently, on a reminiscent evening I checked on line and it's still there. It brings peace and joy to me to know some places that brought me happiness once, still exist and are bringing joy to others.

Our chatty hostess was kindly and helpful. She was exactly what we needed to wrap that day up.

Bowman's Pub was our choice for dinner. These Irish pubs impressed both of us with their abundance of marvelous dark woods, stained glass windows, built-in benches and tables that gave a welcome, cozy feeling. This ambiance would make me feel hungry even if I wasn't, but we both were.

Cups of flavorful Walnut Soup came first to take the edge off our hunger and prepare our palate for what came next. Angelo devoured his lamb chops and I, as much as I loved lamb, went for the chicken breast stuffed with smoked salmon. Baked potatoes came with the dinner, too. We cleaned our plates without any encouragement. This was fine cuisine.

The habit of walking after dinner made me wish we did the same at home. Maybe this trip would start us on a new trend. Many others were walking on this pleasant night, too.

The weather cooperated. No wind. No rain. After some time passed we stopped at a different pub and sat on cushioned, metal tractor seats at the bar. The Irish coffees served to us were the perfect ending to this not-so-perfect day. Irish bartenders were the epitome of making us feel welcome. This fellow did too.

The fireplace gave a sensual, cozy touch to the large room. Old farm tools hung from the stone walls. A curved staircase led to the upper floor. We soaked up every last second before taking that last, easy walk to our B & B.

A gorgeous, sunny morning greeted us. We were going to miss these wonderful Irish breakfasts when we got home, but we certainly enjoyed them while we were here.

On the drive to the Cliffs of Mohr, we passed several stone towers and castle ruins dotting the landscape. They always caught my attention. It was so different of anything I saw in the States.

They led me to think we were stepping into past history. As we pulled into the carpark, it began to drizzle. We had quite a distant walk over hard ground, steps, landings, more steps to more landings as the wind kicked up.

The closer we got to the edge of the Cliffs that stood proudly above the Atlantic Ocean, the windier it got. It blew so hard that it took my shoulder bag off my shoulder! With the luck of the Irish, I caught it before the wind took it away! We really needed our strength to not be blown over! Hail blew *up* from the mists below the Cliffs! Neither of us went closer than 50 feet to the edge. It was too dangerous and neither of us was stupid.

No lingering for us in this place, it was cold and getting wetter. Rain started coming down hard as we hustled back to the car.

An Irish cottage that looked vacant and seemed to need restoring stood nearby. A charming thatched roof needed some attention, reached out to my heart already so full of the Ireland of old and the Ireland of today. A sentimental mood washed over me knowing our stay here was coming to a close.

 Kilkee, a seaside town tucked into a cove was our choice for warmth and lunch at the end of our drive south along the Wild Atlantic Way (as it was named) coastline. Thoughtful, quiet reflection settled over us. Our time in Ireland was running out. We had been so fortunate, all our choices were excellent ones and this town was, too. Now that we were safe, even the Ring of Kerry was much more appreciated.

The pub served a tasty Seafood Chowder to me. Angelo enjoyed his vegetable soup and mussels. Warm, artistically carved woods within complemented the aquarium on the wall. It created perfect, restful ambiance so good for digestion. We were refreshed, renewed, and winding up this last whole day in Ireland. I felt a bit saddened that we were leaving the next day. I knew I would carry this adventurous visit with me always. I loved Ireland.

Angelo had been advised to go to Bunratty Castle. But it appeared too touristy for our taste. Neither one of us was a shopper. We visited real Irish castles and eaten in real Irish pubs, so we could not see the benefit of paying a large fee to visit this one. We did stop in at Dirty Nellie's for a pint, but enjoyed it less than the pubs we stopped in. It was fine for others, just not what we looked for in a visit.

We continued walking the town, stopped to roam at the 12th century Ennis Friary/Abbey ruins. It constantly impressed me how the buildings in Europe were constructed to still remain standing 800 and more years later! Many were just ruins, but even the ruin walls and towers and particular details of swirls and design were intact. The original buildings remained upright showing the superior craft from a time and place thought as inferior. When the age in which they were built was considered, these places were awesome, even the ruins of them!

Even, and especially, the stone bridges that were every bit as old as the castles and cathedrals, and had much more wear and tear on them, were beautiful as well as sturdy structures, many without concrete to hold them in place. The stone was cut to fit. Where has this talent gone?

The only blight on our trip was returning the car to the car rental place. Their representative tried to blame a hole in the spare tire and something about the passenger side view mirror. I guess they thought they were intimidating a little lady alone. (Angelo never stood near at these times.) When I turned belligerent and loud, they backed off and passed the car, returning our deposit in full. This was back in '92; hopefully they have trained their representatives better. This minor incident would not mar the wonderful, adventurous visit to beautiful Ireland!

Our return flight, at 600 miles per hour, took 6½ hours. Probably about the time it took me to drive around the Ring of Kerry!

Unknown to me until we got home, Angelo had slipped a fist-size stone into his pocket that he took from the wall around the mound of Newgrange. He placed it in *my* luggage! I fumed and ranted at him (quite unusual for me) and refused to speak to him for a week. I felt he desecrated a holy site and perhaps brought home some bad energy, not from the stone but by his act of taking it.

He didn't understand my feelings. He had no concept of why I was upset. I told him to mail it back. He didn't. I refused to allow it in our home. He placed it in our flower garden where it remained.

After a week it was laid to rest and soon we would be planning another trip of adventure. Hmm. I wondered where in the world we would go next.

Chapter 22
Finger Lakes, Canandaigua
Finger Lakes, Farmington, New York

"Squaw Island," he said, sounding confident and knowledgeable. "It's unique in the way that oncolites, also known as water biscuits, a light, feathery limestone, are formed here. They crumble when dried.

"If you like American history, you'll want to know, back in the 1780s during the Revolutionary War, Native American women and children found refuge on the island for protection from General John Sullivan's soldiers during his ongoing campaign against the Iroquois Six Nations. I hope I'm not boring you," he took a deep breath.

"Oh, no," I quickly replied glancing at Angelo, not quite certain he was still interested. But he was still engrossed, too.

It was August '94 and time for us to explore our country and neighbor Canada again. Our first stop was Canandaigua, New York at the Canandaigua Lake, one of the Finger Lakes that make this area special. We were standing in the grassy area of a park looking out toward a small island. Angelo started to talk, as he always does, to a fellow also enjoying the view.

The stranger continued. "Native American legend states the Great Spirit was so impressed by the beauty here it blessed the area by laying a hand on it. The fingers made impressions on the ground that filled with water, creating lakes. There is one more for extra measure.

"More of the factual, they were *Keepers of the Western Door of the Iroquois Confederacy*. Their governmental procedures helped form the Articles of Confederation created in 1777 by the 13 Colonies. In addition the matriarchal society and traditions influenced the

147

fight for women's property rights in the mid19th century by the American feminist movement."

Hearing all this from a history enthusiast, proud of where he lived added to my delight in being there. After our friendly fellow ended his history lesson, we lingered, enjoyed the wide, open green spaces.

Angelo asked the man if there was a nearby winery we could visit. We wanted to see the process *the big guys* used to make wine. The man gave us directions and we headed off.

We made 110 gallons of wine a year in the basement of our Victorian apartment house in the middle of downtown Bordentown. The town of 4,000 people sat on the banks of the Delaware River, cocooned by highways going around us.

I ran a gift shop in the front of the building and managed the other five apartments. Our apartment in the back of the building was three stories high and had eight rooms. Angelo's barber shop was catty-corner across the street. We were living an ideal life, happy together.

The basement floor was partial dirt, partial poured concrete. Boulders and large stones were the foundation walls. A typical basement window of approximately 12 inches by eighteen inches was the only source of exterior light.

Angelo charred the inside of each of the barrels. The oak wood softens and smooths the wine to marry together a blend of flavors. A large upright oaken barrel, open at the top sat in the middle of the back room. We drove 40 miles to the Italian Market in Philadelphia to buy wine grapes. Angelo had a troublesome heart, so I lugged the 42 lb. cases of grapes, all eight of them, 80 feet from the front of the building to our *wine room*.

He dumped the grapes from a case into the gadget that worked much like my mother's wringer on her washing machine when I was a kid, turned the handle, squeezing the grapes and stems into the barrel. When it filled, he covered it to steep for three days and we went upstairs to clean up.

The next night, too excited to wait three nights, we went downstairs to check our first step in wine-making. To our horror a line of ants came in through the window (old, old window and frame) crept down the wall, across the floor, up the barrel and into the crushed grapes! The line of ants was constantly moving. YIKES! What could we have done? Egads! We had no idea!

We trudged back upstairs and poured some store bought wine and sat, thinking it wasn't so bad to just buy the wine we drank each night.

The following night we went down the basement steps slowly as if the ants might attack us or something. Afraid to look, we still directed our eyes to the barrel, the floor, the wall, and the window. *Voila!* The ants disappeared! And they never came back!

Our next step was to scoop the pulp out of the barrel and put it into the wine press. The press was like a girdle of wood slats. Angelo would turn the handle around this time, pressing the grapes down tighter and tighter, getting all the juice possible out of the pulp. The juice ran out of the lip, into a bucket which I poured into the smaller, 30 gallon size barrels lying on their sides on a rack Angelo made. The juice from the bottom of the big barrel was placed there, too.

One of the guys that picked up our trash twice a week noted the empty grape cases I set on the curb and caught me at the door.

"I gotta tell ya, I luv wine! I'll be looking for a

bottle come Christmas time!" He laughed heartily, knowing there would be a bottle waiting for him. The town workers were a great bunch.

Actually, all the early morning dog walkers, and those who did not have dogs, and everybody else on the main street knew we were making wine! That's small town living.

With all that homemaking wine in the back of my mind, we found the small, family-owned Finger Lakes winery. The tour was brief but satisfying. Angelo asked questions, got answers and ordered sandwiches which were very plain and sparse. The young man opened a bottle of wine for us, supplied us with plastic glasses, and we happily walked out to the verdant, grassy area under a shade tree. The rows and rows and rows of grapevines growing all around us while we nibbled our lunch and drank wine made right on these grounds, was the perfect setting for us today..

As soon as we finished, we bagged up our leftovers and headed for the racetrack in Farmington. The grounds were beautifully laid out. Lush flowers adorned the middle of the post parade area adding color and glamor to its appearance. The paddock was open for all to watch as the jockeys saddled up and readied the horse for the big moment-the race. I enjoyed standing against the white rail fencing and watching this procedure. Somehow it added to the excitement of the race.

Many of big-name, popular jockeys that were familiar to me, raced here, too. When the races ended for the day, we pointed north to Canada with lots of territory to cover.

Chapter 23
Canada Again, Part 1
Thunder Bay, Grand Casino, Churchill Downs

It took us two hours to reach the Canadian side of Niagara Falls after we left the Canandaigua race track. We spent the night enjoying the Falls lit up, walking around town a bit, getting wet from the spray of the Falls splashing over the low wall, and loving all the flowers that seemed to grow everywhere.

In the morning we cruised around to see the Queen Victoria Park, took a closer look at the 40 feet wide Floral Clock that was surrounded by 38 feet of flowers and plants. I previously read about the Niagara Parks horticulture staff changing the design twice a year while the Ontario Hydro maintained the mechanism. Working together. Wonderful!

These little bits about the care that goes into the flowers displayed in town left a deeper appreciation on me since I was part of beautifying my own home town. I took notes so I could carry ideas back to Bordentown for the improvements many of us wanted to continue making. This included how the hanging baskets were maintained and watered. Enough notes taken, it was time for us to go. We had miles to go ahead of us.

We drove by Barrie in '85 on our way to French River, when we had no time to stop. I noted that we would come by this way again so we could see Barrie. The name intrigued me, as names often did. It was like one Sunday on a dull winter day, I drove 17 miles to Princeton, where a sign *Montague, 85 miles* stood and intrigued me each time I saw it. I took that day to find what Montague looked like and the part of New Jersey I passed through to get there.

I was born and raised in New Jersey, didn't have a clue where Montague was and had never heard anyone mention the name. Curious. I was curious. I found it was at the end of Route 206 which ran approximately 130 miles from Hammonton in the Pine Barrens of South Jersey, through Bordentown, to Trenton the capital of the state, to the beautiful Appalachian Mountains of Montague in the Northwest part of our small state. Simple. I didn't have to be curious any longer.

As far as Barrie went, I noticed somewhere that the town was named for Sir Robert Barrie. Without learning much about him, we at least had a scrumptious lunch at a rather unique Goodfellas on the Kempenfelt Bay.

This restaurant served German, Italian, British, Greek, and CanAm foods. The CanAm being cleverly touted Canadian/American foods. It served breakfast from 1:30 a.m. until 2:30 p.m. Most likely the early hour served as an ending to their featured live entertainment in the evenings.

We were back on the road before long, my curiosity about Barrie satisfied, continued on Hwy 11 to reach North Bay in plenty of time to get a rustic log cabin for the night. The room held a double bed, a night table with a small lamp, a wooden chair, and a TV on a small stand.

Actually we arrived in plenty of time to rent a row boat. The day was so bright, just warm enough that we each lay back and let the boat drift. No one else was around. It was just us on the water. Peaceful. We both slipped into a light sleep.

I woke in a jolt! One glance around told me we had drifted far away from shore! Instantly I remembered Angelo was not a swimmer. He was also easily excitable. A mild panic rose inside me. But he woke easily and just began rowing back. No problem. He wasn't a bit fazed that we were so far from the beach.

As he rowed, I looked down and realized that the water was wide but not deep. If the boat *had* tipped over, we could have waded back to land! Hahaha!

Later that night we turned on the TV to hear Ben, Adam, Hoss, and Little Joe Cartwright of Bonanza fame speaking French at the Ponderosa ranch! It was a repeat experience of Tahiti.

The main street enticed us for a stroll, but mostly we saw huge rocks, trees, and beautiful water. We were 210 miles north of Toronto.

The next morning, we drove even farther north to west along the northern shore of Lake Nipissing, headed for Sudbury. Angelo was getting itchy for a horse race.

He exercised some patience to stop in Sturgeon Falls along the way. He also itched to fish in this place that was all about good fishing. Alas! We had no poles or other equipment and needed licenses, too.

Sturgeon Falls was home to the Nippising Tribe. Trapping, trading, and fishing were their way of life when the first white trapper, Jean Nicolas arrived in the 1620s. A trading post was established near here in the 18th century that became known as Fort La Ronde.

Just west of Sturgeon Falls was a rural area that was settled in the 19th century by Francophones who emigrated from Michigan. They wanted to preserve their French language and culture which was affected by the American people surrounding them in Michigan. Stopping in foreign places that weighed heavy with their past was natural. I let the history vibrate through me before hopping back into the car.

Sudbury came into view a couple hours later. The size of it surprised me. When we were at Sudbury Downs nine years earlier, it appeared to be a small rural town. We must have been on the outskirts of this sprawling city.

The Big Nickel was a fun stop for a photo shoot. The colossal coin was 30 feet in diameter and weighed over 14 tons! It was made and displayed to recognize the nickel miners in Sudbury. At one time they were suppliers of nickel–copper ore to the world.

We were too early for the thoroughbred racing. The track was closed until a grand re-opening was planned for September 10. We expected to be miles away by then.

The following day, at my plea and knowing how far north we were, I suggested that we continued driving north just to see what was there. For five and a half hours, the road took us far north then southwest. We saw no one and no sign of anyone except for several mail boxes lined along the road. It was miles and miles and miles before we saw the next line of mailboxes. Forests were all around with occasional peeks of sun-sparkled water glistening through the trees.

The first sign of people was the town of Chapleau. It appeared to be small. A tiled wall painted with a large, colorful collage of art representing the area stood out in this area of forests and more forests. A railing and walkway wound around it to the top. We had no clue what it was or why it was there. We didn't investigate or ask any of these people walking by us with unapproachable looks on their faces. But I did wonder about it.

We were starving and spotted the only café on the block-long main street. The sign said *Sportsman Hotel and Dining Room*. Nothing fancy. People on the street stopped and stared at us when we got out of the car and watched us

154

walk inside. It was a little unnerving. Again, inside each person stopped what they were doing and looked at us. We both ignored it, smiled, and sat at a formica top table with chrome legs. The sparse interior reminded me of an old 1920s kitchen; well-worn but serviceable. It matched the exterior façade. No one smiled in greeting including our waitress. She was an older woman who looked like her feet hurt. The food offered was plain meat loaf, mashed potatoes, and string beans. When truly hungry basic is more than enough. It was delicious.

Everyone continued to stare at us as we were leaving. They seemed to want to ask what we were doing there! No one said a word. We thought they were all Native Canadians. No one spoke. No one was friendly. There were no open smiling faces. No one was rude either. It was a weird experience I didn't expect as a seasoned traveler.

I recently researched and found that the Sportsman was originally built in 1887 as a classy Queen's Hotel with its own china design two years after the community was established with the arrival of the Canadian-Pacific Railway. Old photos found online showed the Victorian graciousness of the exterior, with balcony. That was long gone when we arrived. The building burned down in 2003 long after we paid the visit.

Chapleau settled by several different Canadian-Native Nations, the Metis Nation and the Francophones. I added it to an interesting out-of-the-way place in my travel book.

Chapter 24
Canada Again, Part 2
Thunder Bay, Grand Casino, Churchill Downs

Our stomachs were full and we were on the road again. We had driven far enough north that we had been in the Artic watershed where all the rivers flowed to the North Pole rather than to the equator. A roadside sign told us so.

Hours later, we came upon a 28 feet high statue of a Canada goose. He stood on the roadside with wings outstretched, ready for flight, extending a welcome to everyone who drove or hitch-hiked across Canada to Wawa. Apparently there were a multitude of hitchhiking stories and the goose floating circulating.

This was a good place to stop. I thought. The name Wawa was intriguing because convenience stores along the east coast of the States carried that logo and name. I had never heard it in any other capacity and now saw it here as a town.

I later learned that the Wawa store name did come from the Ojibwe name for the Canada goose depicting teamwork and encouragement. The store's originator probably had a love of poetry. The name was used in Henry Wadsworth Longfellow's *The Song of Hiawatha.* (A Canada Wawa goose postage stamp was issued in 2010.)

We decided to have a light bite and stretch our legs at the only place we saw open. Formica topped tables and a mix-match of chairs were scattered around a medium sized room. The linoleum floor was a bit warn and dingy, as was the lighting. Nothing fancy or cozy here. No other people eating either.

The small pizza we shared was unlike any pizza we ever ate, but we were out to see and taste other cultures.

Angelo drank two bottles of beer and I drank one. The waitress handed him a check for $40.00! Wow!

Angelo politely questioned it. She explained about an assortment of taxes, special tax on the alcoholic beverage, etc. We had no idea what she was trying to explain. He paid it quietly. We left a bit unhappy with Wawa. *No wonder she didn't greet us with a smile,* I thought. Actually no one smiled the whole time we were in the place.

The Lake Superior northern coastline drive took five hours to reach Thunder Bay, our final destination point before driving south to return home.

Approaching the city we saw a sign that read *Amethyst Mining, pull in here!* Wow! I've loved this semi-precious stone since I found my grandmother Elizabeth's amethyst jewelry in my mother's treasure box. She passed away when I was less than a year old, but I could feel her presence when I held amethyst stones. A lifetime later, her amethyst jewelry still has that effect when I hold them. Thoughts of her are always with me tucked into the back of my heart and mind.

Amethyst was known for opening the Third Eye, clarifying one's spiritual vision. Grandmother Elizabeth was fully developed metaphysically. She read Tarot Cards.

Automatically, the car's steering wheel just turned onto the dirt and pebble road going up a hill to a parking lot where a small, unstable-looking building stood. I thought I heard Angelo say, "okay." I hadn't really asked, knowing he shared my curiousity too.

It felt good to get out of the car to stretch our legs before going inside the weathered building. The lady gave us a little direction on what mining amethysts really meant.

Surprisingly, we didn't have to dig or do anything more strenuous than look on the ground in corners and niches. Amethysts were there for us to find and pick up. She turned us loose in the rocky terrain that spread out beyond the shack.

As I looked around on the ground, the stories of this stone being mystical ran through my mind. I knew ancient Egypt and Greece people believed that amethysts held magical powers, as many continue to believe today, me included. Many mummies uncovered in the tombs of Egypt were adorned with amethyst jewelry.

We scoured the ground, picked up a few stones, larger than a marble, smaller than a golf ball. I kept in mind that the cost was equivalent to the weight of what I chose.

When we went back inside, not knowing anything about the physical properties of the stone, I asked about some pieces being coarse. The lady explained that it was their natural state of some mixtures before polishing. Amethyst is in the crystal quartz group. It was different depending on the area it was found.

Her version of the Thunder Bay legend told about how Chief Nanibijou showed Man where Mother's gold, silver, and amethyst were hidden. His punishment was to lie forever as a sleeping giant on the island in the bay.

She chatted about the cleaning and polishing of amethysts, its history and the many legends surrounding these beautiful purple stones.

A jar of small, polished amethyst gem stones went home with me. Visions of making jewelry and decorative art pieces were dancing around in my head. I loved to create! Since they are known to soothe and heal emotional upsets maybe they would be beneficial to me in the future.

Satisfied with our amethyst excursion we slipped back into the car to look for a motel. After dinner we settled in for the night. It was a tiring, but wonderful day of seeing a part of Canada we hadn't traveled before.

In the morning, after a hearty breakfast, we found Fort William, arriving before any crowds appeared. We wandered around the exteriors of the buildings. I was snapping pictures left and right, happy in my element. A bit of disappointment settled on me. We did not take time to explore the interior of this replica of the Great Rendezvous of the old Northwest Fur Trading Post. Woe was me that I didn't insist. It was unusual for Angelo not to just sit in the car and relax while I explored. I chalked it up to his being anxious to see his family.

Driving around Thunder Bay gave us the feeling of place. We paused waterside, looked out to the island sprawled in Lake Superior, to see that the *Sleeping Giant* of amethyst infamy. He was still lying on the island as condemned to do. A few years later, my friend Tom Moyer, gifted a painting to me that showed the *Sleeping Giant* perfectly. He had no idea when he painted it. But there was no mistaking it for anything else. Each place I moved to, it went with me to hang on my wall and remind me of Thunder Bay. Ah, the mysteries of amethyst!

Angelo called and made arrangements to meet his family. We spent a lovely afternoon at his cousin's home, a reunion for him and new to me. An aunt and uncle, lots of cousins, and in-laws surrounded us with camaraderie and good conversations to get acquainted. Since my family was small with few cousins who never got together, this family's warmth impressed deeply. I felt welcome.

"I've visited my uncle, aunt, and cousins a couple of times over the years." Angelo explained why this part of his family settled here, "My father's brother emigrated to Canada.

There was no food or work in Italy after the war. It was a very hard time." The family was now expecting us.

His uncle led me out to see his handmade hothouse garden explaining how he got a jump on growing his tomatoes because the summer was not long enough. He was proud of his ingenuity.

The cousins invited us to join them at camp the next day. Yikes! Instant panic! I brought no clothes that even resembled outdoor attire for sitting around a campfire, sleeping in tents, or hiking in the woods. Angelo hadn't either.

"Ooops! His cousin said, with a smile spreading across her face. "No need to be upset. The term *camp* is used differently here." It referred to their summer homes up along the lake. Whew! Lucky me.

Their camp was nestled deep in the forest that we drove through for the last week. Their large new, modern house had a long covered porch overlooking the lake. The glistening water was a stone's throw away. The fishing poles were stacked near the dock just waiting to be cast into the water.

We ate, drank, and talked, talked, talked the day away into the night. At bedtime it didn't take but a second to fall into a deep sleep, as sound as a newborn baby, breathing in the natural scent of the forest and pristine waters. It was a wonderful family weekend to put into our memory bank.

On Monday we drove south across the border into Minnesota, sadly saying adieu to Angelo's family and Canada. Wonderful, warm memories came with us to be revisited when we returned home.

Our next point of interest after driving south along the dazzling waters of Lake Superior, seeing the huge boulders of rock jetting out of the ground, was the Grand Casino.

The Mille Lacs Band of Ojibwe Native Americans were the owners, relatively new to gaming in the States. It opened in '92 located half way between the Twin Cities and Duluth, away from the highly traveled route.

Many signs led us deep into the middle of what seemed like miles and miles of cornfields. That was it, cornfields! Finally we saw a huge, sprawling neon-lit casino surrounded by these cornfields like an island in the middle of a green sea.

Casinos don't excite me, so I dropped Angelo off, determined to fill my desire to see nearby Hinckley. Lots of signs about the *Great Hinckley Fire of 1894* dotted the area.

One hundred years ago this entire area was populated by pine trees, hardwoods, and five other, smaller, communities. When the loggers finished devouring the trees they selected, they left behind a multitude of dried, dead stumps of tinder. When sparks started a fire, the heat of the afternoon encouraged a firestorm to create a wall of flame 4 ½ miles high! It swept across the land consuming and destroying all within the area, including those five smaller communities.

Four hundred eighteen people were burned to death unable to outrun the flames! Many more had hidden in ponds or swamps and suffered burned lungs from the intense heat. Smoke-damaged their eyes.

Today's town remembers the heroes of the day in a museum that explained it all.

Angelo was ready to leave when I returned to the casino. It was easy to find him since Monday afternoons were not the busiest times for gambling.

Back on the road again, we loosely planned to stop some distance before entering Chicago to spend the night and visit Arlington Race Track the next day. As we neared Chicago the traffic became crazier than ever. I drove in New York City often and I drove in Rome, Sidney, and Washington D.C., all major, busy city driving. Chicago was worse!

The challenge was not being able to maneuver to get into the lane I needed to be in, to make the turn I needed to make. We also had no clue how to find Arlington Race Track. We saw no signs of horse racing and no street signs to let us know where we were. Plus we would arrive three hours earlier than we needed if we did find the place. Ack!

Angelo said, "Forget it. Let's get out of here." He was not a man of great patience. I was happy to comply.

So we did. Unable to find Arlington we drove to Louisville, Kentucky keeping the famous Churchill Downs on our horizon. I kept in mind that I chose the winner, *Go For Gin*, Chris McCarron up, at the Kentucky Derby earlier that year.

We didn't attend in person, but we made a small celebration of it. The race began after Angelo closed his shop for the day. I made finger foods ready to go with cocktails. We shared the early evening with horse racing friends Joyce and Del Davis and watched it on TV. Hmmm.

Maybe I would be lucky again, I thought. I didn't expect the excitement of a Kentucky Derby Day, or to see ladies in fancy hats and outfits, or to see any horses draped in a horseshoe made from red roses. I certainly didn't expect to see (or their spirits risen from the dead) Harry S. Truman, Jimmy, Rosalyn, and Amy Carter, George and Barbara Bush, Gerald Ford, Richard and Pat Nixon, or Ronald and Nancy Reagan, knowing that they had all attended a Kentucky Derby Day.

It was just cool being in such an internationally famous place!

We stayed the night just north of town. The track was located in the center of a closely built residential area! It appeared the neighborhood grew up around the track. I wondered how the trucks and horse trailers managed to maneuver the narrow streets and sharp corners.

On TV, the entire race track appeared to be a hugely spread-out facility. It is not! It was comparatively small in respect to other tracks we visited. Even the infield seemed tiny. Overall, Churchill Downs did have a cozy feel to it.

We were disappointed. The meet didn't start for a couple weeks. We vowed to go back when the horses were running.

We never did.

Chapter 25
Del Mar
San Diego California

Angelo came up with the idea to fly to Las Vegas in August, rent a car, spend a day before driving to the California coast.

When we sat in the office of the car rental place, I could see by the agent's expression that he assumed we were typical senior citizens coming to Vegas for the coupons and cheap rates. Why else would anyone come in the hottest month of the year when the average temperature is 105 degrees? My impression was reinforced with his "enjoy your stay in Vegas" comment. We didn't offer a word otherwise. He didn't ask, we didn't tell.

I accepted the keys quietly. We cruised the Strip, also to familiarize our location a bit. Circus, Circus was Angelo's choice. I couldn't guess why. It would have been my last choice. But this was Angelo's world. He liked casinos and I liked to see him happy.

After settling in and freshening up, we took the elevator downstairs where the action was happening. Only, there wasn't a lot of action. It *was* August and we *were* in the *desert*. It was pleasant to roam around the casino without thick crowds. We used their gift of coupons, something rare for us to do, for a special meal that didn't impress me as special.

I was off to bed with a book since none of the action interested me. Angelo remained at the gaming tables.

Early the next morning I checked our maps and chose our route to the California coast. It took seven hours of driving US-95 northwest to reach Reno on the border of Nevada and California. We noted, surprisingly, the town was small and unassuming. A good place to stretch our legs. We found a perfect little place in a quiet neighborhood for a bite to eat. It was a welcome change from gaudy Vegas.

Lake Tahoe was less than an hour away. We were not surprised at the beauty here! It was that wild, deeply forested appearance that we saw on the TV Bonanza program, even though the scenes were not filmed there. The Ponderosa, whether the Cartwrights were speaking English, French or Italian had been situated in a great place.

Brrr. The freezing, cold temperature surprised us! In August! We settled in early since we hadn't packed for this weather! The fresh mountain air put us right to sleep under piles of blankets.

A bracing breakfast after that wonderful night of sleep prepared us for the drive on I-80 through the Sierra Nevada mountain range. I'd never been in this area of the country before and was excited about exploring new territory! I kept in mind the sad ending of the pioneers trying to cross the Donner Pass in 1846. Half of the 85 did not make it. Some ate the bodies of their dead friends in order to keep from starving to death. It's enough to make me vegetarian. I paid silent homage as we drove through the area.

As we came down out of the mountains and into a flat area of California, I looked forward to seeing acres of roses (think Rose Parade) as we approached Roseville. I was disappointed. There wasn't a rose bush in sight! None. Zilch.

Our drive continued in the valley toward Vacaville. Gigantic vegetables farms filled both sides of the road like wading through oceans. These were vastly different from the small truck farms I grew up with in New Jersey. We did pass one farm of brilliant yellow flowers, but I couldn't tell what kind they were.

Approaching San Francisco lifted my spirits as high as the suspensions of the Golden Gate Bridge reaching into the sky. Who cared if it was jammed with cars inching from one side to the other? It was exhilarating! No, it was not gold but gleamed as gold when the sun touched it. A bridge known across the world and we were on it! The bridge was mentioned in so many books I'd read and featured in so many movies I'd watched. We drove into San Francisco bumper to bumper with a zillion cars who knew where they were going and I had no clue where to go. I just drove.

As luck would have it, we quickly stumbled onto a small motel of 4 units, one story high, in a residential neighborhood near a park. Amazingly, it was not expensive! We signed for two nights, unpacked, rested about a half hour and set out to find Fisherman's Wharf. I noted the location so we could find our way back without problems.

We were starving. My mouth watered for the Clam Chowder Boule (round ball of sourdough bread with a cap sliced off, bread scooped out, and filled with creamy clam chowder) that I'd read much about.

Found it! Pier 39 was the spot where we could eat in the open air. Angelo bought crab cakes loaded with crab and I savored my long-time-waited-for Clam Chowder Boule. It was thick and creamy, full of clams, tiny potatoes, bits of onion, and lots of flavor. We were both happy and completely sated. (I'd never seen the boule offered anywhere else until the following winter when the corner restaurant in Yardville, four miles up the road from us in Jersey, offered it on their menu. Wonders never cease!)

Fisherman's Wharf was much larger than we expected. Angelo could no longer do a lot of walking so we moseyed back to the car to do some drive-bys.

Steiner Street was first on the list. Many beautifully kept detached Victorian townhouses in cheerful pastel colors lined the street. They were filmed for backdrop in TV series, movies, and novels. These houses were models for the original Shelia's Collectibles. Her three-dimensional wood houses, approximately 5" or 6" high were big sellers in my gift shop. It was satisfying to see the full-size originals in all their glory.

Crazy Lombard Street with its eight hairpin turns on an extremely steep hill one-block long, the crookedest street in the country, denied us entry. It was closed off to traffic because it was deemed a hazard. We did get out of the car to see it from the bottom. Cable cars were also unfamiliar to us so we went to see them rumbling up and down the hills before we drove to Chinatown.

This was another place that was huge compared to what we expected. It would be too much for Angelo to walk so we found a cool, classy bar near the entrance and took a break. The place was near empty which gave us chat time with the bartender. Many art posters and art work were hung on the walls all around the large room.

Behind the bar overlooking the room was an especially beautiful painting of a larger-than-life size cougar. I was much taken with it and took several photos of it. Since we worked up an appetite again, we feasted on fish broiled with herbs and spices before we headed back to the motel for the night.

It felt good the next morning to not pack up to move on. We found a neat neighborhood breakfast place, relaxed, ate, and planned our day. Back to the Golden Gate Bridge area we went, looked across the bay at Alcatraz 1½ miles away, and opted not to spend a day going there. The fog came rolling in warning us to leave. We continued to laze around, poking in here and there, bought some lunch at a deli reeking with delicious scents and picnicked in the park near our motel.

Well, the next morning I *did* know the way to San Jose but decided to take the other road to the enchanting Monterey Peninsula and Carmel-by-the-Sea instead. It's easy to fall in love with places where I could imagine everyone lived a perfect life. The landscaping was full and lush with palm trees, bushes with brightly colored leaves, and flowers everywhere in between.

We found Flaherty's Seafood Bar & Grill on Sixth Avenue and wished every place we stopped would serve the same quality of lunch. Clams, crabs, oysters,calamari, and fish all cooked, I'm certain, to the utmost of taste followed by fabulous desserts. We drooled over the choices. Angelo ordered pasta with clams and the pan seared cod for me. No disappointment here! The flavors and tastes wereas good as anticipated. We ended the meal by sharing a fancy dessert and espresso coffees. We enjoyed espresso coffee at home but had not seen it anywhere since we came away.

Walking off lunch with a short stroll through the storybook village with small, individually-owned shops, all quality and upscale, was a thoroughly enjoyable idea. Tiny, narrow streets were closed off, landscaped, featured gazebos, and sheltered sitting areas with benches showing respect for the visitors who come to see this charming place.

Alas, we had to move on if we were going to reach Del Mar Racetrack in San Diego before we turned east for Las Vegas again. It was another of Angelo's goal racetracks to see personally.

On the side of the highway I spotted a sign for the Hearst Castle and mentioned that I would love to see it.

Surprisingly, Angelo said, "Go ahead."

I knew he didn't realize it would take hours to tour it. The sign didn't say how far away it was. It could have been 60 miles out of our way, or it could have been a mile away. I had no idea of time schedules for tours, etc. so I passed, knowing I'd be sorry when I got home.

It was Saturday. We stopped for the night in Pizmo Beach because it was best to face driving through Los Angeles on a Sunday morning to avoid the horror of traffic I expected from the tales I heard. Why create angst when it was so easy to bypass.

Luckily at 5 p.m. we found the last room available in a small inexpensive motel right on the beach! The beauty of the Pacific Ocean received only a glance or two from us. We were plumb tired after traveling all day.

After that fabulous, extensive lunch in Carmel-by-the-Sea, we settled for a pizza at Del's on Shell Road, recommended by the motel clerk. It was a true Italian pizza as good as we ate in Jersey. And that was good!

A sound night of deep sleep by the ocean readied us for a bracing Sunday morning breakfast under our belts, we pointed in the direction of Route 101 for Los Angeles. I was ready to do battle! The battle that cars, trucks, and every other vehicle known to man, (and California) that I would be negotiating in between, around, and hopefully not under!

The road swelled out and became 10 lanes wide! This was August, '95 and I was stunned! I had never seen a highway that wide! It was a good decision to come through this area on a weekend morning. There was traffic, pulling in and out of lanes, but not the bumper to bumper moving parking lot style as usually reported. I was guessing it was probably the I-5 roadway without seeing any road signs. I

170

just knew I was driving due south to San Diego, hands tense on the wheel, eyes scouting the road signs so I wouldn't miss a turn or make a wrong one. *That* would be murderous to correct!

It worked out fine. We got through LA with a minimum of sweating under pressure. The two hour drive gave us another surprise. San Diego was spread out with wide avenues, one-story houses and lots of palm trees to add to the laid back attitude. After leaving San Francisco with its narrow streets, high buildings and Victorian age of old, San Diego felt youthful.

As *my* usual habit, I drove around aimlessly to get the feel of place before we looked for signs leading us to Del Mar Racetrack. The energy of Angelo's anticipation was charging out to me. I had better find it quick.

Neither the late Bing Crosby (or his spirit) nor any other famous person greeted us at the gate as was his habit in the early days of Del Mar. He came with Pat O'Brien, Gary Cooper, Joe E. Brown, Charles S. Howard (Seabiscuit's owner), and Oliver Hardy to build and open Del Mar Racetrack in 1937.

The Spanish Colonial Revival style was the design choice of architect Sam Hamill to reflect California's history. It gave the track style and distinction; a more intimate feeling. The village of Del Mar became the playground for the movie stars of the day. Many of today's celebrities carry on the tradition. Its slogan *Where the turf meets the surf,* is still sung today.

Plenty of horseracing fans *were* at the gate. I didn't look to see if any were famous. I recognized a few East Coast jockeys, i.e. Chris McCarron, Chris Antley, and Lafitt Pincay, Jr. when I read the program. The fields were larger than we usually saw back east; many with 12 starters. Del

Mar was spread out with lots of space everywhere. Maybe that was why it didn't seem to be as crowded as I would have expected on a Sunday afternoon. The park was beautiful with palm trees and fully blossomed flowers in colorful abundance.

We sauntered to the parade ring which helped make a decision that worked. Seeing the gleem of the horses, the intensity of their expressions, their anticipation for the race held my attention. I also watched the jockeys, looking for a spark to alert me. I scooted to the window. Instinct paid off. Yippee! I won the mile long third race with Princess Afleet, G.F. Almeida up. I giggled to myself.

That was enough to hold me until the sixth race when my cheers and arm waving brought in a favorite. Announce, with Corey Nakatani up. It didn't pay a lot but that was okay. I loved winning, especially on a hunch. I'd never heard of the jockey but took a shot. That's why I read the racing form. A contented smile stayed on my face when we left after the seventh race.

Angelo never told me if he won or lost unless it was a biggie when he needed me to cash his ticket. The walk to the car was a lot slower on the way out than arriving. It always was. Now it was time to turn the car northeast to complete our Las Vegas to San Francisco to San Diego to Las Vegas loop.

Not wanting to retrace our steps, we drove east then north, avoiding LA area traffic. We took secondary roads up the eastern California border, driving through small towns, suburbs, and open countryside. We spent the night in a small motel in a largely residential neighborhood. I was delighted to find a place easily since the day had fallen away and night was fast approaching. There were no other commercial businesses around and few cars. Unusual. I think my travel angel was at work, finding a place and guiding us to it

As usual, we left early the next morning. Before noon Angelo said, "Stop! Stop! Look at that fig tree! I want some of those figs. Pull in the driveway."

The tree branches drooped with figs. It stood on the lawn near the front door of an adobe-style house in the residential neighborhood we were driving through. The houses were set back about 50 feet from the road.

I slowed down, hesitated, then backed up, but I didn't pull into the driveway. That seemed a bit invasive. I pulled to the side of the road in front of the house.

Angelo got out of the car, walked up to the front door, knocked, and asked the lady if he could pick a fig from her beautiful tree. The tree was just ripe with figs! The ground was covered with them, laying there rotting away..

She smiled and said, "Wait, I'll get a bag for you. You can pick as many as you like." She did and he did. He was a happy man.

Angelo was a man who constantly amazed me! I didn't have the courage to do what he just did. He made friends of strangers all the time in the unlikeliest places. I even took a photo of him and the young lady in front of the fig tree whose branches still drooped with fruit after he filled a paper grocery bag. Not the average tourist photo!

Driving through the huge Mohave Desert came next, again surprising us. California seemed to have it all from one extreme to the other. Just over the Nevada border was the Prima Donna Casino in Primm Valley. A giant Ferris wheel looked ludicrous popping up from the desert floor! It was seen miles away. It was a convenient break in our travels but we only stayed long enough to use the rest rooms. Vegas was calling us.

The car rental attendant only glanced briefly at our mileage after looking at what he saw as *two old folks,* commenting that we drove 130 miles. He assumed we never left the Las Vegas area. We had actually driven over 1300 miles! I would have loved to see the expression on his face when he realized that night, how far we had actually driven.

Chapter 26
Italy, Part 1

Volare ran through my head as Dean Martin sang it in 1958 though we were flying to Italy in 1988. *Nel blu di pinto di blu, Let's fly away up to the clouds* still runs through my head now as I write, bringing the memories back to me clear as a bell. The song will probably play in my head for days.

All of Italy lay before us as we landed in Rome, but before we explored Rome, Angelo drove along major highways with beautiful, lush flowers in the dividing aisle between lanes and by the roadside. I was impressed already. Our destination was the ancient mountain town of Soveria Mannelli in Catanzaro, Calabria, southern Italy where he was born and raised. We drove south sometimes in the mountains, sometimes looking out to see them in the distance.

This was all new to me. Exciting to finally see places I read about ever since I could read. For Angelo, it was coming home. His family emigrated to the States in the early 50s when he was a young teenager. He had been back to his home village, but not often and not recently.

We left the highway and drove up, up, up as the road curved leading into town. Stone, concrete and old filled my eyes. Houses were shoulder to shoulder as they usually are in town. It was a sure sign that Soveria Mannelli had been here a long time and wasn't going away anytime soon.

Joyous, happy reunions with family and extended family welcomed us. His brother Sante and wife Irena were there for the summer and also greeted us as if we hadn't just recently spent time together. They welcomed us to their home. I loved it here immediately.

The next day we visited La Sila, a charming mountain-side town where Sante and Irena owned property. Sante filled us in, touching a bit of history.

"This was a favorite vacation spot for high ranking Nazi officers in the 1930s and '40s." He said. "I hated to see them invade our land, bringing their threats dressed up in uniforms. Now I'm happy the area is cleansed of any sign that they were once here."

The area was returned to a pristine setting once again. Covered in pine trees, La Sila was known for the purity of its air. We dined at the Park Hotel surrounded by those dark pine trees on the bank of Lake Avro. These were mountains dressed in pines.

Dishes full of Funghi Risotto and Porchetta placed before us after lingering over the antipasto platter. The taunting scent filled our nostrils as Ciro` vino perfectly accompanied the meal.

We walked after dinner and I bought a lovely chess set of handcrafted wooden pieces and a small tree carved of wood for wall décor. I kept my eye out for unusual items for my gift shop grand opening as soon as I returned home. I especially looked for items small enough to slip into my suitcase. This was a great way to begin our adventure!

Again Sante and Irena joined us the next day. San Giovanni en Firore and Nicastro were towns we rode through heading for Tropea, a jewel in a picture postcard seaside setting, edged by aqua colored water and white beaches. The streets were full of people laughing on this glorious, sunny day. We looked around at a few restaurants before stopping at an open courtyard.

Sante said, "Wait while I check the men's room first. If it's clean, for sure the kitchen was too." We laughed, but we agreed he was right. It passed the test and we sat down. Delicious Rigatoni Tropea-with eggplant, zucchini, black olives and tomatoes, topped with fresh basil was served. Traglia, a local fish with a pink-red skin followed. We bought a bottle of water and a pitcher of vino was placed on the table for us to help ourselves. Interesting. This was so opposite of the States where a pitcher of water was free and diners paid for a bottle of wine.

Angelo and I stopped at a bank to change some dollars to lire (1037 lire for each $1.00). He stepped through the door and the door closed and locked before I could go in! The door in front of him opened and he stepped into the bank. It sort of isolated anyone coming in, one at a time. Leaving was the same. I was certain this would discourage bank robbers. Hmm. Maybe that was the idea?

I'd never seen that before but 20 years later the same set up was in the bank in Littleton, North Carolina where I moved nearby.

Capo Vaticano was our next stop, also by the water's edge showing more sparkling azure water. Tartufa (truffles) grew here where particular dogs were trained to sniff them out of the ground. On the way home I noticed fires burning across the valley on the next mountain over. No rain in the last 7 months yet the vegetation was still lush and green. Tomatoes and vegetables still ripened and were delicious.

Pedivigliano was Irena's hometown, lovely, bursting with flowers everywhere possible. We came away with a full bag of fat, juicy, fresh figs which tasted *nothing* like dried figs! That night we ate dinner, scrumptious lamb with roast potato, et al, at somebody's family's (I was totally confused by now, to know who was related to who and how they were related. The Italian spoken was too fast for me to get it.)

177

Clearly I remember the modern interiors lavish of marble and crystal, completely opposite of the exterior which may be 800 years old! I loved the ancient here. Angelo never seemed to notice, but then he grew up with it.

In Severato, still in Calabria, on the coast of the Ionian Sea, Gulf of Squillace, the four of us visited another relative, the publisher Roberto Rubbertino and wife Rosetta at their condo. I was sorry my Italian couldn't keep up with the conversation flying around the table this Sunday afternoon. I know I would have loved being part of what was being discussed. He graciously gave me several books he published, all in Italian, that I swore I would hover over and study when I got home. Hah.

Before his lovely gift was given, his wife laid the table with an antipasto of chilled fish, calamari, with small mussels on top and fresh slices of lemon throughout. The platter was as pretty as a Gastronomica Food Magazine cover and much more delicious. The wine pitchers passed continually around the table. Then came homemade pasta with fresh pomodoro, followed by a platter of pan fried Triglia, a platter of delicate calamari, squid, and crisp, golden brown, lightly coated eel. Eight of us around the table moaned in pleasure by the time we finished. I could have happily spent a week at that table. But it was better that the beach called to us. To walk after dinner was an Italian tradition. It settles the food and I needed that because I ate too much to be comfortable.

The ride home, in the dark, on narrow mountain roads was a bit scary, but we made it safely.

Sunday was market day when folks gathered in the square, put up tables, some with tents to keep the hot sun off their heads. Fresh fruits, meats, vegetables, and all kinds of things were offered for sale. It was well attended. Angelo ran into several people he knew from his youth.

I spotted the church and asked to go inside.

"Sorry, it's closed for lack of attendance. There aren't enough parishioners to support a full time priest." Sante said.

Wow! I never expected to hear that about any church in Italy! Sante found an old timer that he knew and I got the tour after all. He unlocked the huge, heavy doors to slip inside to a cool interior.

It was beautiful with religious art murals, trimmings in gold and white, the altar was covered with fine cloth, gold crosses, and many candles. It was as if local parishioners just walked out after Sunday Mass and left everything, expecting to return the following Sunday, then didn't. There was some water damage from a leak or two in the ceiling, not near the altar but towards the rear of the church. If I thought a small church in an ancient town would be simple, I was wrong. There was nothing plain about this church. Apparently the younger set were leaving the church too, as I knew they were in the States.

We wandered away after closing and locking the doors again. I asked Angelo about the cemetery. Much history can be found in the cemetery and often beautiful statues and exterior art work. Another surprise for me. This was a mountain town, no stretches of flat land. So the people that made the decisions installed mausoleums but not in a building, just out in the open. The coffins just slid in with information of the person on the front panel. I checked the dates looking for the old ones, there weren't any older than the 1900s.

Again I asked "where are all the old ones?"

Angelo said "after a certain amount of time they are dumped over the side of the mountain."

I was appalled! I wondered if he was telling me the truth or not, but had no one to ask. Generally, he wasn't a man to joke.

An overall glimpse reminded me of the cemeteries of New Orleans, Louisiana. Though, their problem is the high water table of the land, not the rock of a mountain. We managed to slip away one morning to be on our own, just taking in the surrounding mountainous area with no destination or place we had to attend.

Suddenly, we slowed down on the road rolling to a full stop. A herd of sheep surrounded us, their shepherd sauntering along soaking up the sun and enjoying the peace of the day. No one was in a hurry and neither were we. The shepherd wave gently. Angelo acknowledged him.

The image from the picture *To Catch a Thief* with Cary Grant and Grace Kelly came to mind. They, too, were on a country road, surrounded by a herd of sheep. It was a scene cut out of the original movie before it became a DVD, but it always lay in my memory. I think they were going on a picnic and we went on many picnics, just the two of us. I thought it was charming, both in the movie and at the very moment it happened to us.

Another moment still sharp in my memory was when Angelo pulled off the road and encouraged me to walk up to a spout tucked into the side of the mountain. Water flowed from it constantly. A cup sitting on a rock allowed us to sample, cool, clean, refreshing water on this warm summer day. No chemicals, mechanics, money needed, or fuss; just water flowing and delicious. Mother Earth was offering us a taste of her sweet water. My heart burst with love for this place of serenity and this country. This day would last a lifetime for me. I believed no tourist would ever experience this moment as we were.

Before we turned to go back to town and tend to more visits of family and friends, Angelo again parked on the side of the road. He took my hand to lead me where the land dipped down 20 feet from the road edge before the mountain it was, rose up. A little house built on a stone base peeped up just above the dip.

Angelo showed that special smile of his, because he was showing something to me that I'd never seen before. He opened the door to where a statue stood about a foot tall. He looked like a Roman Centurion, without armor, in a painted blue tunic and red cloak. His right arm lifted strait up. A king's crown sat at his right foot. His left arm was bent in front of him, holding his cloak. A coiled snake curled at this left foot.

An empty wine bottle, a red glass with a candle, and a small, red bucket was placed in front of him. Angelo lit the candle and put some lire in the bucket. My mouth dropped open in amazement! You're leaving money here? Anyone could take it! (I'm from New Jersey where no one left money anywhere.)

"That's okay," he said. "Maybe they need it. It's what you do here."

How could I not love him and love it here, the place he was born and raised with traditions different from my own.

The last night in Soveria we dined with Fausta and Alphonzo, niece and nephew to Angelo's brother and wife, Renato and Rafelina. A few years later when they visited the States, I was thrilled to take them for a ride-by tour of Washington, D.C. on a Sunday afternoon.

That night we were welcomed into their condo. The aromas that came to the door with them, told me we were in for another dinner to remember, a memory in the making. Fausta served an ensalata featuring fresh, sliced eggplant, served with good bread (they have the best bread in Italy), homemade spaghetti with fresh pomodoro, lightly fried chicken fillets, roast patate with veal cubes. Her piece` de resistance was a fabulous Trifle brought to the table in a glass pedestal bowl! The wine had been flowing from the pitchers on the table that served the 8 of us. Dinner was ended with espresso and Frangelico. A joyful evening was had by all!

It was good that we did a lot of walking during the day to walk off the fabulous meals. Yet, because the pasta was always freshly made, it was light, not at all like dried pasta we bought in a box at home and served in thick, heavy tomato sauces. I also delighted in the tradition of people coming out after dinner to walk the avenue saying, 'buona sera" as they passed each person and said it again on the return walk to home. I thought it was a lovely way to end the day.

As wonderful as the week was, being treated better than royalty, as celebrities from America, was over. It was time to leave Angelo's childhood memories and extended family, to start exploring Italy. He had not traveled any distance outside Calabria during his previous visits home. Now we would venture together.

Chapter 27
Italy, Part 2

The Isle of Capri *was* a place to fall in love, even if I was in love already. This was the '80s when places were not overcrowded even in the vacation month of August. Capri was at the entrance of the Bay of Naples in the Tyrrhenian Sea, off the fabulous Amalfi Coast where rugged mountains end in Prussian blue water.

The coast is known for its unique, colorful ceramics and their beautifully designed tiles are on display, brightening the area even more than the natural beauty of the place. Shops, restaurants, hotels, etc. exhibit the works of this ceramic art freely on their facades. We shopped in a few places where I purchased some pieces for my soon-to-be-open gift shop. The artist of one pitcher in particular happily posed for a picture. The pitcher still sits on my shelf. I could never part with it. Sometimes profit just takes a back seat.

Yes, we wanted to take the rowboat to the Blue Grotto. Angelo never learned how to swim but never hesitated to go out on a boat. Faith, he must have had a strong faith. But he wouldn't need it on this day. A recent storm made the water choppy so the boats weren't going out.

Even without going to the Blue Grotto, the island was still a magical place that covered me in a glow. I also enjoyed taking a break from our walking, by sitting on a bench that would seat 6 people with ease. It was a completely boxed shape with fancy, white ceramic tiles designed with swirls and flowers artistically done in the style of the Amalfi coast. It was stunning and for the convenience of visitors who took great pleasure in people watching, as I did.

The Gaylord's song "Isle of Capri" from the

'50s played through my head over and over as we strolled the beautiful island under a summer blue sky. Angelo loved the songs of that period too, but his cassettes were all in Italian. So I learned the lyrics in Italian. We sang happily along together.

Our meal at La Roundinella Ristorante was perfect. We worked up quite an appetite as usual and now feasted on crispy Fritta Calamari, freshly made spaghetti, and my favorite Aubergine (eggplant) Parmesan as we overlooked the landscape. We both enjoyed good food, good service, good wine, and a beautiful setting. This place gave all.

An exquisite pitcher, obviously made locally, sat in the middle of the table, filled with local wine for us to pour as much as we liked. It was refilled as we filled our glasses. Forget about fancy labels on bottles, this was definitely a trend I'd love to see in the States.

We reluctantly left the Isle of Capri behind and drove northwest. There was so much to see on our way to Cordenons, near the Slovenia (split from Yugoslavia in 1991.) border. We were going to that northeastern destination to visit Angelo's friend from his youth, but had many stops along the way first.

Our next town to stay was Santa Marinella, north of Roma, where Angelo's Zia Anita owned a restaurant by the sea. We drove around but could not find it from the directions he brought. The next best thing to do was find Il Bettolino, a fine seafood restaurant. It was a drizzly day, but warm so we sat under cover on the terrace and feasted on Insalata de Mare so fresh the taste of the sea popped in my mouth. Tiny clams, shrimp, calamari, squid, a bit of fennel, and celery for crunchiness tossed with thin slices of lemon, olive oil,

184

garlic. The full flavored Rice with Shrimp wafted up a divine aroma. Cold Frescati wine was the perfect mate. Yum. We both loved fresh seafood. We chatted with a young couple from Munich. They both spoke perfect English. Angelo is good at striking up conversations at the table. It's common to do that in Europe. We lingered over fresh fruit served with espresso.

At home Angelo buys a bushel bag of clams from his friend who has his own clam bed. The clams are so fresh the shells are still black. Angelo was fabulous in the kitchen, quick and sure with a clam knife. He knew exactly what to do with them after we had our fill of fresh clams on the half shell. So did that fine restaurant.

We were off again, to drive on pleasant secondary roads to 3,000 year old Montefiascone, Viterbo, Lazio, central Italy, surrounded by high, thick walls of stone and concrete. The streets in town were narrow, steep, and cobblestoned. The town shouted old, old, old. I loved it instantly!

We pulled up to a sign that said *Albergo Dante*. It was just a door with a sign over it. The wall along the street seemed to house the hotel and houses and shops. No fancy front. But, yes, they had one room available in the tower at the top of 36 steps! Yikes!

When we stepped into the albergo, we stood in the cuchina though there was a large glass window on the right. On the other side of it a large, old, thick wooden table was stacked high with freshly made pasta, huge hunks of beef, and stacks of parmigiana cheese.

A woman was making Zuppa Inglese, a fabulous, ancient, Italian dessert of lady fingers dipped in a liqueur, pastry custard, and creamy chocolate, usually served in a glass bowl. The old woman looked up and smiled, a woman obviously happy in her work.

185

Oh, the aromas of an Italian kitchen! And I wasn't even hungry!

I hauled our overnight luggage hoping Angelo would take it slow. I was always concerned about his heart when it came to steps. He was a few behind me. Each step was thick stone. There was one room at the top.....its floor was stone, too. Windows were in each wall, except the one with the steps.

The windows overlooked the red tile rooftops of the town and in the distance, the largest volcanic lake in Europe, Lake Bolsena. I could feel the vibrations of 1,000 people and wondered who slept in this room before us. I could *see* me riding a fast-paced horse; arm raised high, holding a sword, my red cloak flying behind me, my horse's hoof beats clattering over the cobblestones. I wondered what trouble I was in and what year it was then. I had definitely been here in an earlier life lived. I must have been happy because I felt glowing at the moment.

We were in Montefiascone to find Angelo's long-time friend Bellacima. It had turned rainy and we were tired, yet we went searching. It wasn't easy but we found his home in a nook off the main road, sort of like a modern cul-de-sac but old; houses were all connected, dripping history, looking like perfect architecture for this ancient area.

The interior was breath-taking in beauty! The home had marble floors throughout as were the steps to go up to the second floor. Some walls were tiled artistically; a huge vanilla-tinted marble table stood in the kitchen where modern appliances stood. A large fireplace influenced the entire room. A Grundig console sound system with a color TV sat next to it.

Red flocked wallpaper and expensive-looking drapes hung in the living room. A huge entertainment center covered nearly all of one wall, with a bar set-up in it. An espresso machine popped up at a touch. One rounded end had another TV in it.

Bellacima was a pleasant and gracious fellow who didn't recognize Angelo at first. I'm sure Angelo's silver grey hair through him off a bit. He left the States 16 years before we arrived to visit. As soon as he grasped who Angelo was, they slipped into remembering the old days. Soccer played a big part in that. I sat, contented to just listen to the flow of their words, a happiness ran through the conversation.

We didn't stay late. Most importantly, Angelo just wanted to reconnect with his old friend. It meant a lot to him. Angelo was quiet as we drove back to the hotel, probably replaying their conversation, holding it close to him. I didn't ask questions. He would tell me in time what he wanted me to know.

About 40 Italian Navy men were seated at one long table, having dinner among a few others scattered in the long dining room. A feast had been prepared particularly for them. They were a handsome group having a wonderful evening full of joy but not rambunctious.

We were too tired for a full meal but ordered a wonderful Pappardelle Marinara (wide noodle pasta) and Est! Est! Est! wine.

Angelo's brother Sante used to tell the story about the Abbot of a monastery who sent his monk to visit all the inns on the way to the Pope's door in Rome, tasting the wine. If the wine was good, he was to write Est on the door. When he got to Montefiascone he

wrote Est Est Est on the door of the inn! It is understood that when the Abbot arrived at the inn, he was so
happy with the wine that he never did get to see the
Pope. Of course we had to drink this white wine and
carry our own story back home.

We retired early and slept quickly, snuggled in on such
a rainy night after a full, satisfying day. My dreams
were vivid and all mixed up furthering my feeling of
having lived here a long time ago.

A glorious day beheld us, as I looked out from the
balcony window, cool, rain-washed, sunny. I quickly
dressed and ran down the steps, out to the street to the
shop where the street opened up wider. I noticed it the
day before. I bought 2 caffe` and 2 cornetto (croissants)
and ran back up the 36 steps. I loved it here!

We drove through the gates of busy Siena, a walled
town with impressive large statues of Romulus and
Remus at the entrance, then on to Florence. I wanted to
see the original statue of David but we arrived after
siesta was over and the drivers were crazy to get back
to work. They even drove on the sidewalks!
        So I had to be satisfied with the copy of David
by Michelangelo, regal, larger than life; he stood high,
off the road, overlooking magnificent Florence.

We wanted to stay in Greve but couldn't find an
albergo with a room for us. Ten places were filled up.
We drove back to Monteroni D'Arvia within the Siena
provence to a cozy place with fabulous food! We
shared the antipasto and both ordered the Penna
Carbonara made with prosciutto, scrambled eggs and

olive oil. I never had it before. Then we shared fried calamari and shrimp. I had gotten used to the wine always being good. Yum. As usual Angelo struck up a conversation with the next table. They encouraged us to walk in the community after. We did and enjoyed that, too.

We reached Corndenons in the Province of Pordenone, booked into La Cacciatore Albergo which looked very much like an historical Black Forest German hunting lodge. The land in this area is very flat surrounded by snow-capped mountains off in the distance. Everything looks totally different from the rest of Italy we explored. The architecture was different, more German chalets appearing and we see many blondes and many older ladies riding bicycles.

It was time to find Angelo's friend Aldo. We located his sister's house and waited a half hour for Aldo to come home from work.

Angelo and Aldo belonged to the Italian-American Soccer Club in Trenton (NJ) during the 1950s, '60s, etc. The soccer club was very active, even traveling out-of-state to play. Angelo often told me stories of their traveling to games together.

One time they went as a group to New York City for a sports event. When they headed for the train, he lagged behind to pick up a sandwich. When he got to the track there were no steps to go down. His ticket was right. The track number was right, but there were no steps to go down to the train. He went to the ticket window to show that he had a ticket to Trenton.

"There's no steps." He told the guy.

The guy looked at the ticket. He looked at Angelo."The ticket is right. The track is right. The steps appear when the train is taking on passengers."

"How do I get down?'

"No trains run after midnight."

That was it. The guys had run to catch the train and didn't check to see everyone was together. Angelo was left behind and had to take a bus home, arriving in the wee hours of the morning.

Aldo stared at Angelo. It took a minute to recognize him. It had been over13 years since they saw each other. Angelo's hair was mostly silver by now. They were both overjoyed. Memories flowed along with a very good wine with a champagne fizz to it. Aldo had other plans so he couldn't join us for dinner. He was thrilled that his long time friend had remembered him. He encouraged us to drive to Venice, only about an hour south by car.

Back at the albergo dinner was not like our other dinners but delicious, too. We ate a superb radicchio salad, salmon with a white sauce served with spaetzli and white wine in a bottle. No pitchers of wine here.

Most dinners on the menu offered spaetzli or polenta, instead of pasta . The owner greeted us, noting we were American and stated that he had visited Philadelphia the previous year. That was it. He wasn't friendly at all. Poor service followed his seemingly friendly opening. No one else came into the dining room while we were there. It was a chilly place.

The meal reminded me of the story Angelo told me about when he was playing soccer for the Italian-American team. He was very young and associated only with other Italian-Americans. At home they ate foods that were tomato based. Always a dish of pasta along with the main course.

But one time they were playing a game in Massachusetts. The home team treated the visiting team to dinner after the game.

Dinner came out, all on one plate which showed roasted breast of chicken, mashed potatoes with gravy and creamed onions. He and his buddy sitting next to him were shocked! There was not a thing on the plate that had any color to it! He lost his appetite. Everything looked white, pasty, and sickly!

His palate certainly matured since his early days in a new country!

Chapter 28
Italy, Part 3

Venice was an easy, short distance to reach but what greeted us was chaos and noise. Everyone seemed to be bumping into each other and yelling. Angelo insisted I take over, get us onto the boat to cross the canal and secure us a hotel room; even though he was the one who spoke fluent Italian!

I got lucky by getting an English speaking clerk who reserved a room for 2 nights in the Hotel Canale on the first floor (second) overlooking the Grand Canal. I held my breath on the way over because the boat was weighed down with people jammed together like sardines standing up. I thought for sure we would sink during the several stops it had to make before we reached our destination.

We were feeling perky since our drive was so short. We walked and walked then walked some more. I had a map but kept my eyes peeled to find our way. It could be confusing with so many little narrow lanes and bridges over small canals and bridge over the Grand Canal.

We lunched under an awning outside a trattoria. I ate an individual pizza. Angelo foolishly ordered clams on the half shell. I frowned on that since many articles spoke of dirty waters around Venice. It was Saturday and getting crowded with weekenders. We walked again after lunch and found San Marco piazza where we sat over espresso (2 for $12) that included a live orchestra consisting of violin, piano, clarinet, accordion, and base, playing Viennese waltzes and other concert music. It was lovely. The wait staff and the musicians were all dressed in tuxedos. A classic touch. The piazza was not crowded except for the pigeons looking for someone to drop some crumbs for them.

Eventually we strolled over to St. Mark's Basilico, walked up the planks laid out so people could step over the water surrounding the building. It's proof that Venice was sinking. The church had beautiful stained glass windows and statues like all Italy displays. The interior had no pews, just large, cold, empty spaces with people meandering.

Around the corner from the hotel and up the way was Lucia's Trattoria, a small place filled with diners laughing, eating, drinking, and just having the best time. It was just a square, open room but the warmth and camaraderie was mesmerizing. I felt happy and content before I even looked at the menu.

The waiter brought a small cake with a candle to a nearby table. "She said Yes!" he shouted. Everyone cheered with glasses held high to cheer this now-engaged couple. The lady held her left hand high and wiggled it.

As we left Angelo's stomach was upset. I was sure it was the clams from lunch. He wasn't feeling great before reaching here. Afterwards, back at the hotel he encouraged me to go out. It was Saturday night on the Grand Canal! I looked out the window to see five traditional gondoliers formed in a V, glide up the canal, all were singing. Another five followed in the same form and also were singing. It was like being in a live musical Hollywood film!

A bard sauntered up the Calle playing an accordion while he, too, sang. He stopped at table sides

to serenade couples. Happiness dominated tonight-
except in my room where poor Angelo suffered.
Gondoliers drifted back one at a time with lovers
snuggled in their gondolas this time.

In the morning, Angelo, a man who was as energetic as
a live wire, said he was too tired to stroll Venice. We
did walk back to our car, now that we knew we could
without taking a boat across the canal. Now that we
had mastered Venice or at least found our way around
easily, we were leaving. The atmosphere was a lot more
peaceful than when we arrived.

Our next place to visit was Trevi, a walled mountain
town with a castle at the top. I was bursting inside with
excitement! We were going to sleep in a castle tonight!
One much larger than Montefiascone! Wow! The room
was huge, probably 25 x 25 feet! It held a huge,
comfortable bed fit for a king *and* queen. An 8' high,
double door lacquered Oriental armoire and a large,
antique desk sat in the room but the room looked
empty!

This time, I was tired and fell sound asleep early
but woke at that otherworldly hour of 4 a.m. to see a
spider above, on the ceiling, looking down at me! The
ceiling was 25' high too. This was a room I felt lost in.

His body was as big as my thumb with legs long
enough to wrap around a doorknob except this castle
didn't have doorknobs. There was a door pull which
meant no lock. It made me edgy to fall asleep without

the security of a locked door. Now there was this added spider to concern me. I watched him moving toward the wall and I was tired. My eyes closed unwillingly and I fell back to sleep. I guess castles came with spiders, all that stone.

Morning arrived with no spider bites. The shower was my second thought. That room was also large, no fancy gadgets or vanities, just a toilet, tiled walls and a marble floor with a drain in the center of the room. No shower curtain, the water just flowed to the center and went away. No leaks, messy wet floor or moldy curtain. It was the best shower with a great, wide shower head coming down like a spring rain.

It was the first day of school in Italy. As we sipped our coffee and nibbled a croissant, we watched one young lad who was very angry at having to go to school for his apparently, first day. He must have been all of 5 years old.

I drove to Rome jumping into the wild traffic of Rome's everyday craziness. I got smart in a hurry, found a way out of the nutsy atmosphere on the road to Tivoli. It was time for our midday dinner. Whew! A much-needed break before we locate Villa d'Este.

We spent hours walking the beautiful gardens, waterfalls, and fountains, taking lots of photographs of the world famous Tivoli Gardens before finding the Motel River outside the center of Rome, closer to the racetrack. After all the lovely places we stayed, this one was just a plain motel that had a clogged sink. Yuck. At least the room was clean.

The next morning we ventured to take a bus to center city after the girl clerk tells us which one to take and where to get it.

On the bus Angelo told the driver that we have no ticket.

"You tell me?" the driver said abruptly.

Angelo went to the rear of the bus to a little box. He came back to the driver and said, "There are no tickets."

"There are lots of tickets," the driver replied. Angelo was getting frustrated. I was glad to be out of that fast exchange of Italian. I just watched.

Finally a rider told Angelo we must get off the bus, where to buy tickets, then get back on the bus and have the tickets stamped by the machine at the back.

Ohhh. Angelo then explained to me that the last time he was in Italy he purchased tickets directly from the driver. Alas, changes take place all over the world while we are somewhere else.

So we set out to conquer Roma with a smooth hop onto bus #64. The ride itself passed impressive monuments galore, gorgeous fountains everywhere and buildings to match. St Peter's Basilica in Vatican City was an astounding sight to see and even more so to enter. It was elaborately adorned with treasures, art and gold. There was so much gold on the walls and ceilings of the corridor leading to the Sistine Chapel that it all blended together. I was disgusted to see such blatant use of wealth, without the delicacy of taste. I was, however, delighted to see a pair of large, life-size beautiful white porcelain swans on a pedestal. Their simplicity, brilliant, purity stood out like a neon light in darkness. I was double proud because they were a gift from Lenox, a Trenton, New Jersey based company.

Along with the crowds, we inched to the small room of the Sistine Chapel, crammed like a tin of sardines, all craning their necks to see the famous painting of Michelangelo. It was impossible to truly value being there. I could barely breathe waiting to get out of there!

We moved with the crowd to ascend to the rotunda by climbing 336 steps! And I was worried about Angelo climbing 36 steps in Montefiascone! But here, we were nose to someone's rear end. It was slow, one step, wait, one step, wait; in a narrow passageway, barely wide enough to step without turning sideways. Plus the steps were sharply uneven stone! It was smothering without any great reward at the end other than to see over the rooftops of Rome.

I was very unhappy, trapped without being able to do anything about it. I was still filled with rage by the time we retreated to step down, back on the rooftop.

I went to the souvenir shop to buy stamps and post cards while Angelo lit up a cigarette. When I came out, Angelo was nowhere in sight. I looked all over the rooftop. Nothing. I began to panic. There were thousands of people here! How would I ever find him? I decided he must have gone downstairs. I descended in the only elevator, quite upset. I walked around, in and out of groups of people. People were bunched in every space.

Finally I went back to the elevator but was not allowed to go up again. I stumbled trying to think of the word for husband, lost. All that would come out was Spanish, esposa (my wife). The two gendarmes laughed at my mistake; explained that he had to come out of that elevator, there was no other.

For 45 minutes I searched, took time to gaze at the Pieta before returning to the elevator, back to the Pieta again. Very casually Angelo sauntered over to me. I nearly fainted with relief. He was not used to me being angry or upset so I figured he just stayed away from me until I cooled down. It worked. I was back with my feet on the ground, glad to leave the Vatican behind me. All of it.

The best kind of soothing for me was going to Trestevera, the picturesque medieval area of Rome located on the west bank of the Tiber. It escaped redevelopment, thankfully, for our afternoon meal. It was as charming as we anticipated.

We walked down a narrow street to Ristorante da Benito. We feasted on Pasta Porcini Funghi, Lamb with aroma floating up to my nose, and Chi Gaudia (dandelions) with fried hot peppers and garlic; of course, wine.

Ahhh. We were sated and I was happy again.

As we slowly walked back to the bus stop, I stumbled at a 2" high curb and hurt my foot. After all that glory in the restaurant, I'm now in pain finding our way back to Motel River. My foot swells to a scary size when I am standing. I think it cannot be broken as Angelo suggests, because I have a grand opening planned for my gift shop as soon as I get home. What a day!

Angelo sensibly wanted to take me to the hospital. I foolishly refused to admit it may be broken. I told him to go to the racetrack. He did while I just lay with my foot up and read a book; not hard to take at all. We planned to fly back to New Jersey in two days.

Another of Angelo's friends, Adriano and his wife, joined us for dinner. I had not realized how much I missed hearing my own language until we met for dinner. Since they came to the States often and had lived there many years, they both spoke fluent English. It was the perfect ending for our trip. I enjoyed their company and being able to speak my thoughts.

I don't know how I managed to walk into the airporto, to the plane and all the walking after when we landed. My foot continued to swell.

Of course, I went to an orthopedic doctor the day after we arrived home. Two bones in my left foot were broken. He put a walking cast on it. They would have done that just as well in Italy (probably at a much lower cost) and my last few days would have been easier and without pain. My stubbornness is a flaw in my character for sure. I do believe I create my own problems. Sound familiar?

So the Grand Opening of my gift shop still happened on the date it was planned, just with my foot in a cast.

Chapter 29
Ghosts n' Memories Left Behind
Liberty Bell Park
Northeast Philadelphia, Pennsylvania

Liberty Bell Race Track was Angelo's go-to track before we met. He took me there a couple times. Racing in the evening had an altogether different feel to it. Maybe it was the balmy evening atmosphere. The trotters clop, clop created a gentle rhythm which brought the roadway of the Amish to mind. It was so unlike the thoroughbreds thundering hoof sound as they tore down the track in a fury. The wheels of the sulkies made a whoosh sound as if the soft noise of the wind could be heard as they passed by. I liked that sound at Freehold, too, though it struck me differently at night.

It's sad to think the location of that racetrack, offering so many jobs and filled thousands of people with life, laughter, and excitement is now Philadelphia Mills, a mall for big box stores that are the same stores wherever you go in the country. How boring. On a road leading into the mall you can see the only item you'll find to remind you to shout out, "Come on! Come on! You can do it! Keep on coming!" It is named *Liberty Bell Boulevard*.

We often went to Lancaster, home of the Amish community for supper. We feasted on Chicken n' Dumplings, Chicken Pot Pie, Corn Chowder, Amish Roast Beef. Their corn fritters, my favorite always had a dash of creamed corn in the center. I could never figure out how they did that. Their desserts of Shoo Fly Pie and Bread Pudding were fabulous.

We had one favorite restaurant that we returned to each time. Their foods were made with fresh ingredients without all the preservatives used in so many other restaurants. Many of their recipes were still hand made at that time.

Brandywine Raceway
Wilmington, Delaware

Brandywine Raceway was considered one of the prettiest harness racing tracks in the Delaware Valley. Nearly fourteen thousand race fans watched Head Pin as he won the first race in 1953 and collected a Class C pace purse of $900. I wasn't there to see it, but that's how Brandywine Raceway started their record.

I did attend once. It was delightful to watch Hall of Famer Stanly Dancer, hometown driver from New Egypt, New Jersey where I lived at the time. I was familiar with Su Mac Lad, whose picture hung on the American House Tavern & Restaurant wall, had run here too. I tended bar there before moving into the real estate field (later a gift & book shop owner) and many of my customers talked with great pride about Su Mac Lad. It was like hearing about their favorite child making a grand achievement in school.

Hall of Famer Herve Filion was another familiar name that I had seen drive. His name was commonly heard spoken in the tavern because many of the trainers, barn managers, handlers, grooms, etc. were French-Canadian, too. Naturally they would cheer one of their own regardless of where they worked. Brandywine was a top facility that drew big names of standardbred racing.

One remnant left after the last day of racing at Brandywine on Labor Day in 1989 was an old road sign that states *Brandywine*. The upscale housing development that was built after Brandywine Raceway was demolished has street signs that reminded us what once was. Now within the complex you'll find: Sulky Circle, Clubhouse Lane, Derby Way, Bridle Lane, and Trotter Drive. Imitation is a poor replacement.

Garden State Park
Cherry Hill, New Jersey

"The Racetrack of the 21st Century" as dubbed by controversial financier Robert Brennan was a huge disappointment to the working class people who always get the short end of the stick held by hotshots who boast about making it better for everyone. Even as a novice, I knew the first time we sat in the grandstands that an idiot designed the seats for theatre goers who sit down for the show and don't get up until intermission or to leave at the end.

Bettors at a horserace get up out of their seats multiple times during the races. They go to the windows, back to sit, up and betting, out to the paddock, etc. It is a constant movement of the bettor. Theatre goers don't need room between the rows for people moving in and out. In the older grandstands, bettors can walk past a person sitting down without disturbing them or making them stand up so they can pass. A simple observation. A design the architect used to squeeze in more of the "non-elite" in less space so he could lavish space on the jet set. My observation.

To start at the beginning, the track was first opened in '42 while most attention and the great efforts of construction materials were going to World War II. Gas rationing was in. People had to take public transportation to get to the track and none came closer than a mile to Garden State Park. The owner Eugene Mori, provided horse-drawn carts to close the gap from the end-of-the-line public transport to the track as a treat for the fans and as a desperate move on his part, I'm sure.

Garden State Park's location of 7 miles to Philadelphia, where parimutuel betting was unlawful until 1963, proved to be a plum. The open-air grandstand could seat 20,000 race fans. Stables could accommodate at least

1500 horses. During the war years carrier pigeons flew race results to the Philadelphia newspapers within 13 minutes!

In the '60s the tragedy of a father and daughter being crushed to death on an escalator and later when 5 horses burned to death in a stable fire, must have tainted the grounds of this doomed racetrack. I wondered if the track was built on old, sacred Native American burial grounds.

Garden State Race Track hit all the front page headlines when it burned down in 1977 before I had ever even been to a horse race. Two people died in the fire and a fireman suffered a fatal heart attack driving to the fire. It reopened on 1 April 1985 (April Fools' Day!) with big promises (as usual) because it drew Spend a Buck away from the Preakness for a chance to win a $2 million bonus, offered by Brennan if it won the Jersey Derby. Spend a Buck did win with Lafitt Picay up and he did collect $2.6 million.

A follow-up in '88 was one of the greatest harness races, the March of Dimes Trot. A showdown was promoted between American superstar Mack Lobell and French superstar Ourasi. The surprise win was Sugarcane Hanover of Norway.

Angelo had to drag me there with a promise of dinner in a nearby swank restaurant afterward before I would agree to go. I grumbled and growled the few times we went. Nothing *felt* right there and how could I possibly win any money, even though I was still using my $2 bet, when nothing was right? It gave me a feeling of wearing a shirt too tight across my shoulders. The track rattled me. My whole body and mind was askew. I don't remember ever coming home with Garden State money.

Over the years it had hosted some of the best horses in the sport and had top names, including celebrities who came to watch them. It didn't make a lasting difference. The last race held there was May 3, 2001.

A shopping mall and a condo complex was built on the site. The original 1942 gate house remained somewhere on the property unnoticed by most.

Atlantic City Race Course
Mays Landing, New Jersey

We sometimes rode to Atlantic City Race Course on a hot summer week night to catch a couple races. It was not a course I liked and the middle of the work week was inconvenient for me. It was a ride through the truck farms of New Jersey as the earth changed from good farming soil to sand. Today the roadways are filled with strip shopping centers, big box stores, and housing developments.

The track opened in 1946 with John B. Kelly, Sr. as one of the four people to bring it to life. A few of the notable shareholders were Frank Sinatra, Bob Hope, Xavier Cugat, Harry James, and Sammy Kaye.

The attendance fell off after the opening of the nearby casinos and eventually declined seriously until it closed in 2015. *The Sport of Kings* would not be present here anymore.

Chapter 30
Return to Philadelphia Park

An odd feeling came over me on February 2, '97. Yet it was a beautiful, cool and clear Sunday morning. Breakfast at Oliver- a bistro, warmed my stomach but could not settle my restlessness. Angelo passed away in June '96. I was missing him. Feeling that empty space next to me was still present.

I decided to go to the track! My destination was Philadelphia Park where I had spent so many Sundays (and Mondays) over the previous 15 years. Maybe it would settle another loose end and bring some closure to me. The car knew the way even though it had been nearly a year since I'd driven the still familiar route.

As soon as I arrived, I made my way to the location in the grandstand where we always sat. Frank and Fran were sitting there, as if they were still saving seats for Angelo and me, like they had always done. It was briefly as if this past year had not crashed and changed my life. They were delighted to see me and made it feel like old times.

I picked Teleconference with Victor Molina up in the first race and he won! Good beginning! A favorite came in for the second race. The horse I chose in that race did nothing; not even close. The third race was a repeat. It showed me zero. Hmmm. I never had *the touch* Angelo had, but this was disastrous. *Maybe I should just leave*, I thought. *Maybe this was not such a good idea after all.*

It was time to go down to the paddock area to watch the routine before heading to the betting window. Female jockeys always got my attention first. I was pulling for them doing their best to make it in a man's field. I knew personally what a struggle that was. Most of the work I did over the years was in a male-dominated field.

I watched as the trainer saddled up the horse, gave Jocson last minute instructions before giving her a leg up.

She walked around the ring twice, then the escort pony sidled next to her and paraded onto the track, to warm the horse's muscles.

Without a second thought, I slipped over to the betting window and placed Win and Place bets on Safeway Sandy, Gwen Jocson up. It was a long shot, on a 6 furlong race, but I *felt* this bet, felt it was the horse to back. They jogged across the track to enter the starting gate where the gate crew took over leading the horses into the gate and keeping them calm. As soon as all the horses seemed settled, the starter hit the button to open the gates. They were off and running!

I went down to stand by the rail for a clear view of the finish line. My heart was pumping, my hands clutching the program. I felt so sure about this one! Yes, she was keeping up with the pack! She moved up! They ran along the backstretch! The pack thundered around to the fourth turn, the horses gave their all, stretched out, looking gorgeous, flat out running for the wire! I yelled all the way! Hands in the air waved vibrantly! Yowl! She did it! She did it!

Bingo! Jocson came in and paid $188 and $54! I was ecstatic! Angelo must have been looking over my shoulder and guided me to the window. I was certain of it. He appeared at home and gave me signs that he was alive in the afterworld, so why not here?

I treated myself to a delicious hot dog with sauerkraut and mustard. It was still as good as I remembered.

In later years I read where Gwen Jocson retired from racing in 1999. She developed serious brain injuries from the several concussions she suffered during her racing career. She was a fourth generation South Carolina-born and raised girl where the women were once expected to be feminine, genteel, and meek. By her own admission she had to overcome male prejudice, loneliness, poverty, spinal surgery, a broken neck, and multiple other injuries.

She returned for one last race in 2010, which she won. That was atop *Honor In Peace* for the $30,000 allowance race, Legends for the Cure race for retired female jockeys at Pimlico Race Course. Eight female jockeys competed in the *Susan G. Komen Breast Cancer Cure* benefit. Gwen Jocson is another one of the feminine heroes in my book.

Frank and Fran were happy for me, too, even if they didn't go for Jocson. I skipped Races 5 and 6 to study Race 7. I loved the name of City Lady and went for it. Eric Jones was up on this 6 furlong race. He was a new name to me. I stood at the rail and yelled, "C'mon! C'mon! C'mon! You can do it!" And she did! She paid $23 for my $2. I was happy with that. Another long shot, just not as long as Safeway Sandy.

Now I was ready for Race 8 which was a mile long run. Gwen Jocson was riding Imperial Sass. How could I pass up this female jockey who had come from a dirt poor background and had been showing the world she could ride as well as any male jockey?

Can she really win again? I pondered on that. *Well, after all it was the horse running, not the jockey,* I answered my own thoughts.

I was hoping the beautiful thoroughbred was as sassy as her name. Again, she was not a favorite, but I yelled just as loud to bring 'er in! Now I knew Angelo was with me because Jocson brought Imperial Sass to the finish line and paid $14 for my $2.

Enough! I skipped the last race as we often did in previous years. Whew! This was a super good day *running with the horses.* I missed Angelo but somehow this day brought him closer to me again.

It was my first day at the track since he passed away and I had no plans on returning.

Acknowledgements

Many thanks go to Dr. Donald Arnold for reading and giving honest opinions and suggestions.

Much appreciation goes to the Sandra Martin for her professional thoughts, helpful feedback, and encouragement.

Multitude of thanks to Joyce Lindenmuth who read, made suggestions, edited, and guided me to bring so much more to my story. Any errors are my own.

Deep appreciation goes to each person who extended courtesy and welcome to us in all of our travels. There were many and it encouraged me to continue traveling, to see the world and the wonderful people in it even after Angelo passed away.

Horse racing is a dangerous business. My healing thoughts go out to all jockeys, male and female, who suffer serious injuries, yet ride because they love the sport. To the horses, I send blessings for they love the competition and the chance to show what they can do.

Other Books by the Author

Arcadia Publishing
Bordentown
New Egypt & Plumsted
Bordentown Revisited
Bordentown Post Cards with Patti DeSantis

Guy Arlen Publishing
Ghosts of Bordentown

Schiffer Publishing
Haunted Bordentown

PurpleStone Press
Living with Ghosts
The Afternoon Crowd
Major Fraser's
Life & Labyrinth
Ghostly Spirits of Warren Co.NC & Beyond
A Nosegay of Violets
Simply Put
Ghosts Along the Border

Anthologies as Editor

As the Day Dawns
Heartspeak
Seasons
Insights, Outsights
What it is to be a Woman
What If ?
Jane Austen
Tuesday Afternoon

Fir Trees, Spanish Moss, Palm Trees

Arlene S. Bice is the author of more than a dozen non-fiction books on New Jersey history, memoir, metaphysics, and poetry. Her poems *A Writer's Pandemic* and *New Orleans* were performed in the *Pandemic Blues* at the Kirby Theatre directed by Fred Motley in Roxboro, North Carolina. She is the recipient of the Florence Poets Society *Poet of Distinction Award*, published in several anthologies, and is an award-winning artist. The Second Annual Oakley Hall Literary Award was presented to her in 2018.

She assists others in independent publishing and leads two writing groups. Pre-pandemic she hosted *Poetry in Nature* afternoons in the garden at Backyard Birds and the Rosemont Vineyard.

Ms. Bice is a co-founding member of the Warren Artists Market (WAM) and holds memberships in Triangle Association of Freelancers (TAF), Nonfiction Authors Association (NFAA), and International Women's Writing Guild (IWWG).

She holds Life time memberships in the Bordentown Historic Society (NJ) and New Egypt Historic Society (NJ)

Ms Bice is the former proprietor of the By the Book @ U & I Gift Shop (NJ) for nearly 20 years and wrote a book review column for the Register-News for 10 years.

She is an avid reader and serious genealogist that lives in South Hill, Virginia with her bossy cat Captain Midnight. Website: arlenebice.com

Made in the USA
Middletown, DE
19 March 2022